THE

POETICAL WORKS

OF

THOMAS HOOD.

WITH SOME

ACCOUNT OF THE AUTHOR.

IN FOUR VOLUMES.

VOLUME IV.

BOSTON:
LITTLE, BROWN AND COMPANY.
NEW YORK: BLAKEMAN AND MASON.
M.DCCC.LXIII.

RIVERSIDE, CAMBRIDGE:
STEREOTYPED AND PRINTED BY
H. O. HOUGHTON AND COMPANY.

CONTENTS.

VOL. IV.

LOVE AND LUNACY.

THE Moon — who does not love the silver moon,
  In all her phantasies and all her phases?
Whether full-orbed in the nocturnal noon,
  Shining in all the dewdrops on the daisies,
  To light the tripping Fairies in their mazes,
Whilst stars are winking at the pranks of Puck:
  Or huge and red, as on brown sheaves she
    gazes;
Or new and thin, when coin is turned for luck;—
Who will not say that Dian is a Duck?

But, oh! how tender, beautiful, and sweet,
  When in her silent round, serene, and clear,
By assignation loving fancies meet,
  To recompense the pangs of absence drear!
  So Ellen, dreaming of Lorenzo, dear,
But distant from the city mapped by Mogg,
  Still saw his image in that silver sphere,
Plain as the Man with lantern, bush, and dog,
That used to set our ancestors a-gog.

And so she told him in a pretty letter,
  That came to hand exactly as Saint Meg's
Was striking ten — eleven had been better;
  For then he might have eaten six more eggs,

And both of the bedevilled turkey-legs,
With relishes from East, West, North, and South ;
Draining, beside, the teapot to the dregs ;
Whereas a man, whose heart is in his mouth,
Is rather spoilt for hunger and for drouth.

And so the kidneys, broiling hot, were wasted ;
The brawn — it never entered in his thought ;
The grated Parmesan remained untasted ;
The potted shrimps were left as they were bought,
The capelings stood as merely good for nought,
The German sausage did not tempt him better,
Whilst Juno, licking her poor lips, was taught
There 's neither bone nor skin about a letter,
Gristle, nor scalp, that one can give a setter.

Heaven bless the man who first devised a mail !
Heaven bless that public pile which stands concealing
The Goldsmiths' front with such a solid veil !
Heaven bless the Master, and Sir Francis Freeling,
The drags, the nags, the leading or the wheeling,
The whips, the guards, the horns, the coats of scarlet,
The boxes, bags, those evening bells a-pealing !
Heaven bless, in short, each posting thing, and varlet,
That helps a Werter to a sigh from Charlotte.

So felt Lorenzo as he oped the sheet,
Where, first, the darling signature he kissed,
And then, recurring to its contents sweet
With thirsty eyes, a phrase I must enlist,
He *gulped* the words to hasten to their gist;
In mortal ecstasy his soul was bound —
When, lo! with features all at once a-twist,
He gave a whistle, wild enough in sound
To summon Faustus's Infernal Hound!

Alas! what little miffs and tiffs in love,
A snubbish word, or pouting look mistaken,
Will loosen screws with sweethearts hand and glove,
O! love, rock firm when chimney-pots were shaken,
A pettish breath will into huffs awaken,
To spit like hump-backed cats, and snarling Towzers!
Till hearts are wrecked and foundered, and forsaken,
As ships go to Old Davy, Lord knows how, sirs,
While heaven is blue enough for Dutchman's trowsers!

"The moon 's at full, love, and I think of you" —
Who would have thought that such a kind P. S.
Could make a man turn white, then red, then blue,
Then black, and knit his eyebrows and compress

His teeth, as if about to effervesce
Like certain people when they lose at whist!
So looked the chafed Lorenzo, ne'ertheless,
And, in a trice, the paper he had kissed
Was crumpled like a snowball in his fist!

Ah! had he been less versed in scientifics,
More ignorant, in short, of what is what:
He ne'er had flared up in such calorifics;
But he *would* seek societies, and trot
To Clubs — Mechanics' Institutes — and got
With Birkbeck — Bartley — Combe — George Robins — Rennie,
And other lecturing men. And had he not
That work, of weekly parts, which sells so many,
The Copper-bottomed Magazine — or "Penny?"

But, of all learned pools whereon, or in,
Men dive like dabchicks, or like swallows skim,
Some hardly damped, some wetted to the skin,
Some drowned like pigs when they attempt to swim,
Astronomy was most Lorenzo's whim,
('Tis studied by a Prince amongst the Burmans;)
He loved those heavenly bodies which, the Hymn
Of Addison declares, preach solemn sermons,
While waltzing on their pivots like young Germans.

Night after night, with telescope in hand,
  Supposing that the night was fair and clear,
Aloft, on the house-top, he took his stand,
  Till he obtained to know each twinkling sphere
  Better, I doubt, than Milton's "Starry Vere;"
Thus, reading thro' poor Ellen's fond epistle,
  He soon espied the flaw — the lapse so sheer
That made him raise his hair in such a bristle,
And like the Boatswain of the Storm-Ship whistle.

"The moon 's at full, love, and I think of thee,"—
  "Indeed! I 'm very much her humble debtor,
But not the moon-calf she would have me be,
  Zounds! does she fancy that I know no better?"
  Herewith, at either corner of the letter
He gave a most ferocious, rending pull; —
  "O woman! woman! that no vows can fetter,
A moon to stay for three weeks at the full!
By Jove; a very pretty cock-and-bull!

"The moon at full! 'twas very finely reckoned!
  Why so she wrote me word upon the first —
The twelfth, and now upon the twenty-second —
  Full! — yes — it must be full enough to burst!
  But let her go — of all vile jilts the worst" —
Here with his thumbs he gave contemptuous snaps,
  Anon he blubbered like the child that 's nursed
And then he hit the table frightful raps,
And stamped till he had broken both his straps.

"The moon 's at full — and I am in her thought —
No doubt: I do believe it in my soul!"
Here he threw up his head, and gave a snort
Like a young horse first harnessed to a pole:
"The moon is full — ay, so is this d—d bowl!"
And, grinning like the sourest of curmudgeons,
Globe — water — fishes — he dashed down the whole,
Strewing the carpet with the gasping gudgeons;
Men do the strangest things in such love-dudgeons.

"I fill her thoughts — her memory's vice-gerent?
No, no,— some paltry puppy — three weeks old —
And round as Norval's shield"— thus incoherent
His fancies grew as he went on to scold;
So stormy waves are into breakers rolled,
Worked up at last to mere chaotic wroth —
This — that — heads — tails — thoughts jumbled uncontrolled
As onions, turnips, meat, in boiling broth,
By turns bob up, and splutter in the froth.

"Fool that I was to let a baby face —
A full one — like a hunter's — round and red —
Ass that I am, to give her more a place
Within this heart"— and here he struck his head.
"'Sdeath, are the Almanac-compilers dead?

But no —'tis all an artifice — a trick,
  Some newer face — some dandy under-bred —
Well — be it so — of all the sex I 'm sick!"
Here Juno wondered why she got a kick.

"'The moon is full'— where 's her infernal
    scrawl?
  'And you are in my thought: that silver ray
Will ever your dear image thus recall'—
  My image? Mine! She 'd barter it away
  For Pretty Poll 's on an Italian's tray!
Three weeks, full weeks,— it is too plain — too
    bad —
  Too gross and palpable! Oh cursed day!
My senses have not crazed — but if they had —
Such moons would worry a Mad Doctor mad!

"O Nature! Wherefore did you frame a lip
  So fair for falsehood? Wherefore have you
    drest
Deceit so angel-like?" With sudden rip
  He tore six new buff buttons from his vest,
  And groped with hand impetuous at his breast,
As if some flea from Juno's fleecy curls
  Had skipped to batten on a human chest,
But no — the hand comes forth, and down it hurls
A lady's miniature beset with pearls.

Yet long upon the floor it did not tarry,
  Before another outrage could be planned:

Poor Juno, who had learned to fetch and carry,
  Picked up and brought it to her master's hand,
  Who seized it, and the mimic feature scanned;
Yet not with the old loving ardent drouth,
  He only saw in that fair face, so bland,
Look how he would at it, east, west, north, south,
A moon, a full one, with eyes, nose, and mouth.

"I 'll go to her,"— herewith his hat he touched,
  And gave his arm a most heroic brandish;
"But no — I 'll write"— and here a spoon he clutched,
  And rammed it with such fury in the standish,
  A sable flood, like Niger the outlandish,
Came rushing forth — O Antics and Buffoons!
  Ye never danced a caper so ran-dan-dish;
He jumped, thumped — tore — swore, more than ten dragoons
At all nights, noons, moons, spoons, and pantaloons!

But soon ashamed, or weary, of such dancing,
  Without a Collinet's or Weippert's band,
His rampant arms and legs left off their prancing,
  And down he sat again, with pen in hand,
  Not fiddle-headed, or King's-pattern grand,
But one of Bramah's patent Caligraphics;
  And many a sheet it spoiled before he planned
A likely letter. Used to pure seraphics,
Philippics sounded strangely after Sapphics

Long while he rocked like Yankee in his chair,
   Staring as he would stare the wainscot through,
And then he thrust his fingers in his hair,
   And set his crest up like a cockatoo ;
   And trampled with his hoofs, a mere Yahoo :
At last, with many a tragic frown and start,
   He penned a billet, very far from doux,
'Twas sour, severe — but think of a man's smart
Writing with lunar caustic on his heart !

The letter done and closed, he lit his taper,
   And sealing, as it were, his other mocks,
He stamped a grave device upon the paper,
   No Cupid toying with his Psyche's locks,
   But some stern head of the old Stoic stocks —
Then, fiercely striding through the staring streets,
   He dropt the bitter missive in a box,
Beneath the cakes, and tarts, and sugared treats,
In Mrs. Smelling's window-full of sweets.

Soon sped the letter — thanks to modern plans,
   Our English mails run little in the style
Of those great German wild-beast caravans,
   Eil-wagens — tho' they do not " go like *ile*,"—
   But take a good twelve minutes to the mile —
On Monday morning, just at ten o'clock,
   As Ellen hummed "The Young May Moon"
      the while,
Her ear was startled by that double knock
Which thrills the nerves like an electric shock !

Her right hand instantly forgot its cunning,
And down into the street it dropt, or flung,
Right on the hat and wig of Mr. Gunning,
The jug that o'er her ten-week-stocks had hung;
Then down the stairs by twos and threes she sprung,
And through the passage like a burglar darted.
Alas! how sanguine are the fond and young—
She little thought, when with the coin she parted
She paid a sixpence to be broken-hearted!

Too dear at any price — had she but paid
Nothing and taken discount, it was dear;
Yet, worthless as it was, the sweet-lipped maid
Oft kissed the letter in her brief career
Between the lower and the upper sphere,
Where, seated in a study bistra-brown,
She tried to pierce a mystery as clear
As *that* I saw once puzzling a young clown —
"Reading Made Easy," but turned upside down.

Yet Ellen, like most misses in the land,
Had sipped sky blue, through certain of her teens,
At one of those establishments which stand
In highways, byeways, squares, and village-greens;
'Twas called "The Grove," — a name that always means
Two poplars stand like sentries at the gate —
Each window had its close Venetian screens

And Holland blind, to keep in a cool state
The twenty-four Young Ladies of Miss Bate.

But when the screens were left unclosed by chance,
The blinds not down, as if Miss B. were dead,
Each upper window to a passing glance
Revealed a little dimity white bed;
Each lower one a cropped or curly head;
And thrice a week, for soul's and health's economies,
Along the road the twenty-four were led,
Like coupled hounds, whipped in by two she-dominies
With faces rather graver than Melpomene's.

And thus their studies they pursued: — On Sunday,
Beef, collects, batter, texts from Dr. Price;
Mutton, French, pancakes, grammar — of a Monday;
Tuesday — hard dumplings, globes, Chapone's Advice;
Wednesday — fancy-work, rice-milk (no spice);
Thursday — pork, dancing, currant-bolsters, reading;
Friday — beef, Mr. Butler, and plain rice;
Saturday — scraps, short lessons and short feeding,
Stocks, back-boards, hash, steel-collars, and good breeding.

From this repertory of female learning,
Came Ellen once a quarter, always fatter!
To gratify the eyes of parents yearning.
'Twas evident in bolsters, beef, and batter,
Hard dumplings, and rice-milk, she did not smatter,
But heartily, as Jenkins says, "demollidge;"
But as for any learning, not to flatter,
As often happens when girls leave their college,
She had done nothing but grow out of knowledge.

At Long Division sums she had no chance,
And History was quite as bad a balk;
Her French it was too small for Petty France,
And Priscian suffered in her English talk:
Her drawing might be done with cheese or chalk;
As for the globes — the use of the terrestrial
She knew when she went out to take a walk,
Or take a ride; but, touching the celestial,
Her knowledge hardly soared above the bestial.

Nothing she learned of Juno, Pallas, Mars;
Georgium, for what she knew, might stand for Burgo,
Sidus, for Master: then, for northern stars,
The Bear she fancied did in sable fur go,
The Bull was Farmer Giles's bull, and, ergo,
The ram the same that butted at her brother;
As for the Twins, she only guessed that Virgo,

From coming after them, must be their mother;
The Scales weighed soap, tea, figs, like any other.

As ignorant as donkeys in Gallicia,
  She thought that Saturn, with his Belt, was but
A private, may be, in the Kent Militia;
  That Charles's Wain would stick in a deep rut,
  That Venus was a real Wèst-End slut —
O, Gods and Goddesses of Greek Theogony!
  That Berenice's Hair would curl and cut,
That Cassiopëia's Chair was good Mahogany,
Nicely french-polished,—such was her cosmogony!

Judge, then, how puzzled by the scientifics
  Lorenzo's letter came now to dispense;
A lizard, crawling over hieroglyphics,
  Knows quite as much of their Egyptian sense;
  A sort of London fog, opaque and dense,
Hung over verbs, nouns, genitives, and datives;
  In vain she pored and pored, with eyes intense,
As well is known to oyster-operatives,
Mere looking at the shells won't open natives.

Yet mixed with the hard words, so called, she found
  Some easy ones that gave her heart the staggers;
Words giving tongue against her, like a hound
  At picking out a fault — words speaking daggers.

The very letters seemed, in hostile swaggers,
To lash their tails, but not as horses do,
Nor like the tails of spaniels, gentle waggers,
But like a lion's, ere he tears in two
A black, to see if he is black all through.

With open mouth, and eyeballs at full stretch,
She gazed upon the paper sad and sorry,
No sound— no stir — quite petrified, poor wretch !
As when Apollo, in old allegory,
Down-stooping like a falcon, made his quarry
Of Niobe, just turned to Purbeck stone ;
In fact, since Cupid grew into a worry,
Judge if a suing lover, let alone
A lawyer, ever wrote in such a tone.

" Ellen, I will no longer call you mine,
That time is past, and ne'er can come again ;
However other lights undimmed may shine,
And undiminishing, one truth is plain,
Which I, alas ! have learned,— that love can wane.
The dream is passed away, the veil is rent,
Your heart was not intended for my reign ;
A sphere so full, I feel, was never meant
With one poor man in it to be content.

" It must, no doubt, be pleasant beyond measure,
To wander underneath the whispering bough
With Dian, a perpetual round of pleasure.

Nay, fear not,— I absolve of every vow,—
Use,— use your own celestial pleasure now,
Your apogee and perigee arrange.
Herschel might aptly stare and wonder how,
To me that constant disk has nothing strange —
A counterfeit is sometimes hard to change.

"O Ellen! I once little thought to write
Such words unto you, with so hard a pen;
Yet outraged love will change its nature quite,
And turn like tiger hunted to its den —
How Falsehood trips in her deceits on men!
And stands abashed, discovered, and forlorn!
Had it been only cusped — but gibbous — then
It had gone down, but Faith drew back in scorn,
And would not swallow it — without a horn!

"I am in occultation,— that is plain:
My culmination 's past,— that 's quite as clear.
But think not I will suffer your disdain
To hang a lunar rainbow on a tear.
Whate'er my pangs, they shall be buried here;
No murmur,— not a sigh,— shall thence exhale:
Smile on,— and for your own peculiar sphere
Choose some eccentric path,— you cannot fail,
And pray stick on a most portentous tail!

"Farewell! I hope you are in health and gay;
For me, I never felt so well and merry —
As for the bran-new idol of the day,

Monkey or man, I am indifferent — very!
Nor e'en will ask who is the Happy Jerry;
My jealousy is dead, or gone to sleep,
But let me hint that you will want a wherry,
Three weeks' spring-tide, and not a chance of neap,
Your parlors will be flooded six feet deep!

"O Ellen! how delicious was that light
Wherein our plighted shadows used to blend,
Meanwhile the melancholy bird of night —
No more of that — the lover 's at an end.
Yet if I may advise you, as a friend,
Before you next pen sentiments so fond,
Study your cycles — I would recommend
Our Airy — and let South be duly conned,
And take a dip, I beg, in the great Pond.

"Farewell again! it is farewell forever!
Before your lamp of night be lit up thrice,
I shall be sailing, haply, for Swan River,
Jamaica, or the Indian land of rice,
Or Boothia Felix — happy clime of ice!
For Trebizond, or distant Scanderoon,
Ceylon, or Java redolent of spice,
Or settling, neighbour of the Cape baboon,
Or roaming o'er — The Mountains of the Moon!

"What matters where? my world no longer owns
That dear meridian spot from which I dated
Degrees of distance, hemispheres, and zones,

A globe all blank and barren and belated:
What matters where my future life be fated?
With Lapland hordes, or Koords or Afric peasant,
A squatter in the western woods located,
What matters where? My bias, at the present,
Leans to the country that reveres the Crescent!

"Farewell! and if forever, fare thee well!
As wrote another of my fellow-martyrs:
I ask no sexton for his passing-bell,
I do not ask your tear-drops to be starters,
However I may die, transfixed by Tartars,
By Cobras poisoned, by Constrictors strangled,
By shark or cayman snapt above the garters,
By royal tiger or Cape lion mangled,
Or starved to death in the wild woods entangled,

"Or tortured slowly at an Indian stake,
Or smothered in the sandy hot simoom,
Or crushed in Chili by earth's awful quake,
Or baked in lava, a Vesuvian tomb,
Or dirged by syrens and the billows' boom,
Or stiffened to a stock mid Alpine snows,
Or stricken by the plague with sudden doom,
Or sucked by Vampyres to a last repose,
Or self-destroyed, impatient of my woes.

"Still fare you well, however I may fare,
A fare perchance to the Lethean shore,

Caught up by rushing whirlwinds in the air,
Or dashed down cataracts with dreadful roar:
Nay, this warm heart, once yours unto the core,
This hand you should have claimed in church or minster,
Some cannibal may gnaw"—she read no more—
Prone on the carpet fell the senseless spinster,
Losing herself, as 'twere, in Kidderminster!

Of course of such a fall the shock was great,
In rushed the father, panting from the shop,
In rushed the mother, without cap or tête,
Pursued by Betty Housemaid with her mop;
The cook to change her apron did not stop,
The charwoman next scrambled up the stair,—
All help to lift, to haul, to seat, to prop,
And then they stand and smother round the chair,
Exclaiming in a chorus, "Give her air!"

One sears her nostrils with a burning feather,
Another rams a phial up her nose;
A third crooks all her finger-joints together,
A fourth rips up her laces and her bows,
While all by turns keep trampling on her toes,
And, when she gasps for breath, they pour in plump
A sudden drench that down her thorax goes,

As if in fetching her — some wits so jump —
She must be fetched with water like a pump!

No wonder that thus drenched, and wrenched, and galled,
As soon as possible, from syncope's fetter
Her senses had the sense to be recalled,
"I 'm better — that will do — indeed I 'm better,"
She cried to each importunate besetter;
Meanwhile, escaping from the stir and smother,
The prudent parent seized the lover's letter,
(Daughters should have no secrets with a Mother)
And read it thro' from one end to the other.

From first to last, she never skipped a word —
For young Lorenzo of all youths was one
So wise, so good, so moral she averred,
So clever, quite above the common run —
She made him sit by her, and called him son;
No matrimonial suit, e'en Duke's or Earl's,
So flattered her maternal feelings — none!
For mothers always think young men are pearls,
Who come and throw themselves before their girls.

And now, at warning signal from her finger,
The servants most reluctantly withdrew,
But list'ning on the stairs contrived to linger;

For Ellen, gazing round with eyes of blue,
At last the features of her parent knew,
And, summoning her breath and vocal powers,
"O, mother!" she exclaimed — "O, is it true —
Our deăr Lorenzo"— the dear name drew showers —
"*Ours*," cried the mother, "pray don't call him ours!

"I never liked him, never, in my days!"
["O yes — you did"— said Ellen with a sob,]
"There always *was* a something in his ways —
["So sweet — so kind," said Ellen, with a throb,]
"His very face was what I call a snob,
And, spite of West-end coats and pantaloons,
He had a sort of air of the swell mob;
I 'm sure when he has come of afternoons
To tea, I 've often thought — I 'll watch my spoons!"

"The spoons!" cried Ellen, almost with a scream,
"O cruel — false as cruel — and unjust!
He that once stood so high in your esteem!"
"He!" cried the dame, grimacing her disgust,
"I like him? — yes — as anybody must

An infidel that scoffs at God and Devil:
Didn't he bring you Bonaparty's bust?
Lord! when he calls I hardly can be civil —
My favourite was always Mr. Neville.

"Lorenzo? — I should like, of earthly things,
To see him hanging forty cubits high;
Doesn't he write like Captain Rocks and Swings?
Nay, in this very letter, bid you try
To make yourself particular, and tie
A tail on — a prodigious tail! — O, daughter!
And don't he ask you down his area — fie!
And recommend to cut your being shorter,
With brickbats round your neck in ponds of water?"

Alas! to think how readers thus may vary
A writer's sense! — What mortal would have thought
Lorenzo's hint about Professors Airy
And Pond to such a likeness could be brought!
Who would have dreamt the simple way he taught
To make a comet of poor Ellen's moon,
Could furnish forth an image so distraught,
As Ellen, walking Regent Street at noon,
Tailed — like a fat Cape sheep, or a raccoon?

And yet, whate'er absurdity the brains
May hatch, it ne'er wants wet-nurses to suckle it;

Or dry ones, like a hen, to take the pains
  To lead the nudity abroad, and chuckle it;
  No whim so stupid but some fool will buckle it
To jingle bell-like on his empty head,
  No mental mud — but some will knead and
    knuckle it,
And fancy they are making fancy-bread; —
No ass has written, but some ass has read.

No dolts could lead if others did not follow 'em.
  No Hahnémann could give decillionth drops,
If any man could not be got to swallow 'em;
  But folly never comes to such full stops.
  As soon, then, as the Mother made such swaps
Of all Lorenzo's meanings, heads and tails,
  The Father seized upon her malaprops —
"My girl down areas — of a night! 'Ods nails!
I'll stick the scoundrel on his area-rails!

"I will! — as sure as I was christened John!
  A girl — well-born — and bred,— and schooled
    at Ditton —
Accomplished — handsome — with a tail stuck on!
  And chucked — Zounds! — chucked in horse-
    ponds like a kitten;
I wish I had been by when that was written!" —
And doubling to a fist each ample hand,
  The empty air he boxed with, a-la-Bitton,
As if in training for a fight, long planned,
With Nobody — for love — at No Man's Land!

"I'll pond — I'll tail him!" — in a voice of thunder
He recommenced his fury and his fuss,
Loud, open-mouthed, and wedded to his blunder,
Like one of those great guns that end in buss.
"I'll teach him to write ponds and tails to us!"
But while so menacing this-that-and-t'others,
His wife broke in with certain truths, as thus:
"Men are not women — fathers can't be mothers,—
Females are females" — and a few such others.

So saying, with rough nudges, willy-nilly,
She hustled him outside the chamber-door,
Looking, it must be owned, a little silly;
And then she did as the Carinthian boor
Serves (Goldsmith says) the traveller that's poor:
Id est, she shut him in the outer space,
With just as much apology — no more —
As Boreas would present in such a case,
For slamming the street door right in your face.

And now, the secrets of the sex thus kept,
What passed in that important tête-à-tête
'Twixt dam and daughter, nobody except
Paul Pry, or his Twin Brother, could narrate —
So turn we to Lorenzo, left of late,
In front of Mrs. Snelling's sugared snacks,
In such a very waspish stinging state —

But now at the Old Dragon, stretched on racks,
Fretting, and biting down his nails to tacks;

Because that new fast four-inside — the Comet,
  Instead of keeping its appointed time,
Had deviated some few minutes from it,
  A thing with all astronomers a crime,
  And he had studied in that lore sublime;
Nor did his heat get any less or shorter
  For pouring upon passion's unslaked lime
A well-grown glass of Cogniac and water,
Mixed stiff as starch by the Old Dragon's daughter.

At length " Fair Ellen " sounding with a flourish,
  The Comet came all bright, bran new, and smart:
Meanwhile the melody conspired to nourish
  The hasty spirit in Lorenzo's heart,
  And soon upon the roof he " topped his part,"
Which never had a more impatient man on,
  Wishing devoutly that the steeds would start
Like lightning greased,— or, as at Ballyshannon
Sublimed, " greased lightning shot out of a cannon ! "

For, ever since the letter left his hand,
  His mind had been in vacillating motion,
Dodge-dodging like a flustered crab on land,
  That cannot ask its way, and has no notion,

If right or left leads to the German Ocean —
Hatred and Love by turns enjoyed monopolies,
Till, like a Doctor following his own potion,
Before a learned pig could spell Acropolis,
He went and booked himself for our metropolis.

"O, for a horse," or rather four,— "with wings!"
For so he put the wish into the plural —
No relish he retained for country things,
He could not join felicity with rural, [mural.
His thoughts were all with London and the
Where architects — not paupers — heap and *pile* stones;
Or with the horses' muscles, called the crural,
How fast they could macadamize the milestones
Which passed as tediously as gall or bile stones.

Blind to the picturesque, he ne'er perceived
In Nature one artistical fine stroke;
For instance, how that purple hill relieved
The beggar-woman in the gipsy-poke,
And how the red cow carried off her cloak;
Or how the aged horse, so gaunt and gray,
Threw off a noble mass of beech and oak!
Or, how the tinker's ass, beside the way,
Came boldly out from a white cloud — to bray!

Such things have no delight for worried men,
That travel full of care and anxious smart;
Coachmen and horses, are your artists then;

Just try a team of draftsmen with the Dart,
Take Shee, for instance, Etty, Jones, and Hart,
Let every neck be put into its noose,
Then tip 'em on the flank to make 'em start,
And see how they will draw! — Four screws let loose
Would make a difference — or I'm a goose!

Nor cared he more about the promised crops,
If oats were looking up, or wheat was laid,
For flies in turnips, or a blight in hops,
Or how the barley prospered or decayed;
In short, no items of the farming trade,
Peas, beans, tares, 'taters, could his mind beguile;
Nor did he answer to the servant-maid,
That always asked at every other mile,
"Where do we change, Sir?" with her sweetest smile.

Nor more he listened to the Politician,
Who lectured on his left, a formal prig,
Of Belgium's, Greece's, Turkey's sad condition,
Not worth a cheese, an olive, or a fig;
Nor yet unto the critic, fierce and big,
Who, holding forth, all lonely, in his glory,
Called one a sad bad Poet — and a Whig,
And one, a first-rate proser — and a Tory;
So critics judge, now, of a song or story.

Nay, when the coachman spoke about the 'Leger,
   Of Popsy, Mopsy, Bergamotte, and Civet,
Of breeder, trainer, owner, backer, hedger,
   And nags as right, or righter than a trivet,
   The theme his cracked attention could not rivet;
Though leaning forward to the man of whips,
   He seemed to give an ear,—but did not give it,
For Ellen's moon (that saddest of her slips,
Would not be hidden by a "new Eclipse

If any thought e'er flitted in his head
   Belonging to the sphere of Bland and Crocky,
It was to wish the team all thorough-bred,
   And every buckle on their backs a jockey:
   When spinning down a steep descent, or rocky,
He never watched the wheel, and longed to lock it;
   He liked the bolters that set off so cocky:
Nor did it shake a single nerve, or shock it,
Because the Comet raced against the Rocket.

Thanks to which rivalry, at last the journey
   Finished an hour and a quarter under time,
Without a case for surgeon or attorney,
   Just as St. James's rang its seventh chime,
And now, descending from his seat sublime,
   Behold Lorenzo, weariest of wights,
   In that great core of brick, and stone, and lime,
Called England's heart—but which, as seen of nights,
Has rather more the appearance of its lights.

Away he scudded — elbowing, perforce,
Thro' cads, and lads, and many a Hebrew worrier,
With fruit, knives, pencils,— all dirt cheap of course,
Coachmen, and hawkers of the Globe and "Currier;"
Away! — the cookmaid is not such a skurrier,
When, fit to split her gingham as she goes,
With six just striking on the clock to hurry her,
She strides along with one of her three beaux,
To get well placed at "Ashley's"— now Ducrow's.

"I wonder if her moon is full to-night!"
He muttered, jealous as a Spanish Don,
When, lo! — to aggravate that inward spite,
In glancing at a board he spied thereon
A playbill for dramatic folks to con,
In letters such as those may read, who run,
"'KING JOHN'— O yes, — I recollect King John!
'My Lord, they say five moons'—*five* moons! — well done!
I wonder Ellen was content with one!

"Five moons—all full!—and all at once in heav'n!
She should have lived in that prolific reign!"
Here he arrived in front of number seven,
Th' abode of all his joy and all his pain;
A sudden tremor shot through every vein,

He wished he 'd come up by the heavy wagon,
  And felt an impulse to turn back again,
O, that he ne'er had quitted the Old Dragon!
Then came a sort of longing for a flagon.

His tongue and palate seemed so parched with drouth,—
  The very knocker filled his soul with dread,
As if it had a living lion's mouth,
  With teeth so terrible, and tongue so red,
  In which he had engaged to put his head.
The bell-pull turned his courage into vapor,
  As though 'twould cause a shower-bath to shed
Its thousand shocks, to make him sigh and caper—
He looked askance, and did not like the scraper.

"What business have I here? (he thought) a dunce,
  A hopeless passion thus to fan and foster,
Instead of putting out its wick at once;
  She 's gone—it 's very evident I 've lost her,—
  And to the wanton wind I should have tossed her—
Pish! I will leave her with her moon, at ease,
  To toast and eat it, like a single Gloster,
Or cram some fool with it, as good green cheese,
Or make a honey-moon, if so she please.

"Yes—here I leave her," and as thus he spoke,
  He plied the knocker with such needless force,
It almost split the pannel of sound oak;

And then he went as wildly through a course
Of ringing, till he made abrupt divorce
Between the bell and its dumbfounded handle,
Whilst up ran Betty, out of breath and hoarse,
And thrust into his face her blown-out candle,
To recognize the author of such scandal.

Who, presto! cloak, and carpet-bag to boot,
Went stumbling, rumbling, up the dark one pair,
With other noise than his whose "very foot
Had music in 't as he came up the stair:"
And then with no more manners than a bear,
His hat upon his head, no matter how,
No modest tap his presence to declare,
He bolted in a room, without a bow,
And there sat Ellen, with a marble brow!

Like fond Medora, watching at her window,
Yet not of any Corsair bark in search,—
The jutting lodging-house of Mrs. Lindo,
"The Cheapest House in Town" of Todd and Sturch,
The private house of Reverend Doctor Birch,
The public-house, closed nightly at eleven,
And then that house of prayer, the parish church,
Some roofs, and chimneys, and a glimpse of heaven,
Made up the whole look-out of Number Seven.

Yet something in the prospect so absorbed her,
She seemed quite drowned and dozing in a dream;
As if her own beloved full moon still orbed her,
Lulling her fancy in some lunar scheme,
With lost Lorenzo, may be, for its theme —
Yet when Lorenzo touched her on the shoulder,
She started up with an abortive scream,
As if some midnight ghost, from regions colder,
Had come within his bony arms to fold her.

" Lorenzo ! " — " Ellen ! " — then came " Sir ! " and " Madam ! "
They tried to speak, but hammered at each word,
As if it were a flint for great Mac Adam;
Such broken English never else was heard,
For like an aspen leaf each nerve was stirred,
A chilly tremor thrilled them through and through,
Their efforts to be stiff were quite absurd,
They shook like jellies made without a due
And proper share of common joiner's glue.

" Ellen! I 'm come — to bid you — fare — farewell,"
They thus began to fight their verbal duel;
" Since some more hap — hap — happy man must dwell "—
" Alas — Loren — Lorenzo! — cru — cru — cruel! "

For so they split their words like grits for gruel.
At last the Lover, as he long had planned,
Drew out that once inestimable jewel,
Her portrait, which was erst so fondly scanned,
And thrust poor Ellen's face into her hand.

"There — take it, Madam — take it back I crave,
The face of one — but I must now forget her,
Bestow it on whatever hapless slave
Your art has last enticed into your fetter —
And there are your epistles — there! each letter!
I wish no record of your vow's infractions,
Send them to South — or Children — you had better —
They will be novelties — rare benefactions
To shine in Philosophical Transactions!

"Take them — pray take them — I resign them quite!
And there 's the glove you gave me leave to steal —
And there 's the handkerchief, so pure and white
Once sanctified by tears, when Miss O'Neill —
But no — you did not — cannot — do not feel
A Juliet's faith, that time could only harden!
Fool that I was, in my mistaken zeal!
I should have led you,— by your leave and pardon —
To Bartley's Orrery, not Covent Garden!

"And here 's the birthday ring — nor man nor devil
Should once have torn it from my living hand,
Perchance 'twill look as well on Mr. Neville;
And that — and that is all — and now I stand
Absolved of each dissevered tie and band —
And so farewell, till Time's eternal sickle
Shall reap our lives; in this, or foreign land
Some other may be found for truth to stickle
Almost as fair — and not so false and fickle!"

And there he ceased: as truly it was time,
For of the various themes that left his mouth,
One half surpassed her intellectual climb:
She knew no more than the old Hill of Howth
About that "Children of a larger growth,"
Who notes proceedings of the F. R. S.'s;
Kit North, was just as strange to her as South,
Except the south the weathercock expresses,
Nay, Bartley's Orrery defied her guesses.

Howbeit some notion of his jealous drift
She gathered from the simple outward fact,
That her own lap contained each slighted gift;
Though quite unconscious of his cause to act
So like Othello, with his face unblacked;
"Alas!" she sobbed, "your cruel course I see,
These faded charms no longer can attract;
Your fancy palls, and you would wander free,
And lay your own apostasy on me!

"*I*, false! — unjust Lorenzo! — and to *you!*
  O, all ye holy gospels that incline
The soul to truth, bear witness I am true!
  By all that lives, of earthly or divine —
  So long as this poor throbbing heart is mine —
I false! — the world shall change its course as soon!
  True as the streamlet to the stars that shine—
True as the dial to the sun at noon,
True as the tide to 'yonder blessed moon!'"

And as she spoke, she pointed through the window,
  Somewhere above the houses' distant tops,
Betwixt the chimney-pots of Mrs. Lindo,
  And Todd and Sturch's cheapest of all shops
  For ribbons, laces, muslins, silks, and fops; —
Meanwhile, as she upraised her face so Grecian,
  And eyes suffused with scintillating drops,
Lorenzo looked, too, o'er the blinds venetian,
To see the sphere so troubled with repletion.

"The Moon!" he cried, and an electric spasm
  Seemed all at once his features to distort,
And fixed his mouth, a dumb and gaping chasm —
  His faculties benumbed and all amort —
  At last his voice came, of most shrilly sort,
Just like a sea-gull's wheeling round a rock —
  "Speak! — Ellen! — is your sight indeed so short!

The Moon! — Brute! savage that I am, and
block!
The Moon! (O, ye Romantics, what a shock!)
Why that 's the new Illuminated Clock!"

THOSE EVENING BELLS.

"I 'D BE A PARODY."

THOSE Evening Bells, those Evening Bells,
How many a tale their music tells,
Of Yorkshire cakes and crumpets prime,
And letters only just in time! –

The Muffin-boy has passed away,
The Postman gone — and I must pay,
For down below Deaf Mary dwells,
And does not hear those Evening Bells.

And so 'twill be when she is gone,
That tuneful peal will still ring on,
And other maids with timely yells
Forget to stay those Evening Bells.

LINES

TO A FRIEND AT COBHAM.

'Tis pleasant, when we 've absent friends,
Sometimes to hob and nob 'em
With Memory's glass — at such a pass
Remember me at Cobham!

Have pigs you will, and sometimes kill,
But if you sigh and sob 'em,
And cannot eat your home-grown meat,
Remember me at Cobham!

Of hen and cock, you 'll have a stock,
And death will oft unthrob 'em,—
A country chick is good to pick —
Remember me at Cobham!

Some orchard trees of course you 'll lease,
And boys will sometimes rob 'em,
A friend (you know) before a foe —
Remember me at Cobham!

You 'll sometimes have wax-lighted rooms,
And friends of course to mob 'em,
Should you be short of such a sort,
Remember me at Cobham!

LINES

ON THE CELEBRATION OF PEACE.

BY DORCAS DOVE.

AND is it thus ye welcome Peace!
From Mouths of forty-pounding Bores?
O cease, exploding Cannons, cease!
Lest Peace, affrighted, shun our shores!

Not so the quiet Queen should come;
But like a Nurse to still our Fears,
With Shoes of List, demurely dumb,
And Wool or Cotton in her Ears!

She asks for no triumphal Arch;
No Steeples for their ropy Tongues;
Down, Drumsticks, down, She needs no March,
Or blasted Trumps from brazen Lungs.

She wants no Noise of mobbing Throats
To tell that She is drawing nigh:
Why this Parade of scarlet Coats,
When War has closed his bloodshot Eye?

Returning to Domestic Loves,
  When War has ceased with all its Ills,
Captains should come like sucking Doves,
  With Olive Branches in their Bills.

No need there is of vulgar Shout,
  Bells, Cannons, Trumpets, Fife, and Drum,
And Soldiers marching all about,
  To let Us know that Peace is come.

O mild should be the Signs and meek,
  Sweet Peace's Advent to proclaim!
Silence her noiseless Foot should speak,
  And Echo should repeat the same.

Lo! where the Soldier walks, alas!
  With Scars received on foreign Grounds;
Shall we consume in colored Glass
  The Oil that should be poured in Wounds?

The bleeding Gaps of War to close,
  Will whizzing Rocket-Flight avail?
Will Squibs enliven Orphans' Woes?
  Or Crackers cheer the Widow's Tale?

THE LAMENT OF TOBY,

THE LEARNED PIG.

" A little learning is a dangerous thing."— POPE.

O HEAVY day! O day of woe!
  To misery a poster,
Why was I ever farrowed — why
  Not spitted for a roaster?

In this world, pigs, as well as men,
  Must dance to fortune's fiddlings,
But must I give the classics up,
  For barley-meal and middlings?

Of what avail that I could spell
  And read, just like my betters,
If I must come to this at last,
  To litters, not to letters?

O, why are pigs made scholars of?
  It baffles my discerning,
What griskins, fry, and chitterlings,
  Can have to do with learning.

Alas ! my learning once drew cash,
  But public fame 's unstable,
So I must turn a pig again,
  And fatten for the table.

To leave my literary line
  My eyes get red and leaky ;
But Giblett doesn't want me *blue*,
  But red and white, and streaky.

Old Mullins used to cultivate
  My learning like a gard'ner ;
But Giblett only thinks of lard,
  And not of Doctor Lardner !

He does not care about my brain
  The value of two coppers,
All that he thinks about my head
  Is, how I 'm off for choppers.

Of all my literary kin
  A farewell must be taken,
Good-by to the poetic Hogg !
  The philosophic Bacon !

Day after day my lessons fade,
  My intellect gets muddy ;
A trough I have, and not a desk,
  A sty — and not a study !

Another little month, and then
  My progress ends, like Bunyan's;
The seven sages that I loved
  Will be chopped up with onions!

Then over head and ears in brine
  They'll souse me, like a salmon,
My mathematics turned to brawn,
  My logic into gammon.

My Hebrew will all retrograde,
  Now I'm put up to fatten;
My Greek, it will all go to grease;
  The Dogs will have my Latin!

Farewell to Oxford! — and to Bliss!
  To Milman, Crowe, and Glossop,—
I now must be content with chats,
  Instead of learned gossip!

Farewell to "Town!" farewell to "Gown!'
  I've quite outgrown the latter,—
Instead of Trencher-cap my head
  Will soon be in a platter!

O why did I at Brazen-Nose
  Rout up the roots of knowledge?
A butcher that can't read will kill
  A pig that's been to college!

For sorrow I could stick myself,
  But conscience is a clasher;
A thing that would be rash in man,
  In me would be a rasher!

One thing I ask — when I am dead,
  And past the Stygian ditches —
And that is, let my schoolmaster
  Have one of my two flitches:

'Twas he who taught my letters so
  I ne'er mistook or missed 'em,
Simply by *ringing* at the nose,
  According to *Bell's* system.

TO A BAD RIDER.

I.

Why, Mr. Rider, why
  Your nag so ill indorse, man?
To make observers cry,
  You 're mounted, but no horseman?

II.

With elbows out so far,
  This thought you can't debar me —
Though no Dragoon — Hussar —
  You 're surely of the army!

III.

I hope to turn M. P.
  You have not any notion,
So awkward you would be
  At "seconding a motion!"

MY SON AND HEIR.

I.

My mother bids me bind my heir,
But not the trade where I should bind;
To place a boy — the how and where —
It is the plague of parent-kind!

II.

She does not hint the slightest plan,
Nor what indentures to indorse;
Whether to bind him to a man,
Or, like Mazeppa, to a horse.

III.

What line to choose of likely rise,
To something in the Stocks at last,—
"Fast bind, fast find," the proverb cries,
I find I cannot bind so fast!

IV.

A Statesman James can never be;
A Tailor? — there I only learn
His chief concern is cloth, and he
Is always cutting his concern.

V.

A Seedsman? — I'd not have him so;
A Grocer's plum might disappoint;
A Butcher? — no, not that — although
I hear "the times are out of joint!"

VI.

Too many of all trades there be,
Like Peddlers, each has such a pack;
A merchant selling coals? — we see
The buyer send to cellar back.

VII.

A Hardware dealer? — that might please,
But if his trade's foundation leans
On spikes and nails, he won't have ease
When he retires upon his means.

VIII.

A Soldier? — there he has not nerves,
A Sailor seldom lays up pelf:
A Baker? — no, a baker serves
His customer before himself.

IX.

Dresser of hair? — that 's not the sort;
A joiner jars with his desire —
A Churchman? — James is very short,
And cannot to a church aspire.

X.

A Lawyer? — that 's a hardish term!
A Publisher might give him ease,
If he could into Longman's firm,
Just plunge at once "in medias Rees."

XI.

A shop for pot, and pan, and cup,
Such brittle Stock I can't advise;
A Builder running houses up,
Their gains are stories — may be lies!

XII.

A Coppersmith I can't endure —
Nor petty Usher A, B, C-ing;
A Publican no father sure,
Would be the author of his being!

XIII.

A Paper-maker? — come he must
To rags before he sells a sheet —
A Miller? — all his toil is just
To make a meal he does not eat.

XIV.

A Currier? — that by favor goes —
A Chandler gives me great misgiving —
An undertaker? — one of those
That do not hope to get their living!

XV.

Three Golden Balls? — I like them not;
An Auctioneer I never did —
The victim of a slavish lot,
Obliged to do as he is bid!

XVI.

A Broker watching fall and rise
Of stock? — I'd rather deal in stone: —
A Printer? — there his toils comprise
Another's work beside his own.

XVII.

A Cooper? — neither I nor Jem
Have any taste or turn for that,—
A Fish retailer? — but with him,
One part of trade is always flat.

XVIII.

A Painter? — long he would not live, —
An Artist's a precarious craft —
In trade Apothecaries give,
But very seldom take, a draught.

XIX.

A Glazier? — what if he should smash!
A Crispin he shall not be made —
A Grazier may be losing cash,
Although he drives "a roaring trade."

XX.

Well, something must be done! to look
On all my little works around —
James is too big a boy, like book,
To leave upon the shelf unbound.

XXI.

But what to do? — my temples ache
From evening's dew till morning's pearl,
What course to take my boy to make —
O could I make my boy — a girl!

THE POET'S FATE.

What is a modern Poet's fate?
To write his thoughts upon a slate; —
The Critic spits on what is done,—
Gives it a wipe,— and all is gone.

DECEMBER AND MAY.

"Crabbed Age and Youth cannot live together."
SHAKSPEARE.

I.

SAID Nestor, to his pretty wife, quite sorrowful one day,
"Why, dearest, will you shed in pearls those lovely eyes away?
You ought to be more fortified;" — "Ah, brute, be quiet, do,
I know I 'm not so fortyfied, nor fiftyfied, as you!

II.

"O, men are vile deceivers all, as I have ever heard,
You 'd die for me, you swore, and I — I took you at your word.
I was a tradesman's widow then — a pretty change I 've made;
To live, and die, the wife of one, a widower by trade!"

III.

"Come, come, my dear, these flighty airs declare, in sober truth,

You want as much in age, indeed, as I can want
in youth;
Besides, you said you liked old men, though now
at me you huff."
"Why, yes," she said, "and so I do — but you 're
not old enough!"

IV.

"Come, come, my dear, let's make it up, and have
a quiet hive;
I'll be the best of men,— I mean — I'll be the
best *alive!*
Your grieving so will kill me, for it cuts me to the
core." —
"I thank ye, Sir, for telling me — for now I'll
grieve the more!"

MORAL REFLECTIONS ON THE CROSS OF ST. PAUL'S.

THE man that pays his pence, and goes
Up to thy lofty cross, St. Paul,
Looks over London's naked nose,
Women and men:
The world is all beneath his ken,
He sits above the *Ball.*

He seems on Mount Olympus' top,
Among the Gods, by Jupiter! and lets drop
His eyes from the empyreal clouds
On mortal crowds.
Seen from these skies,
How small those emmets in our eyes!
Some carry little sticks — and one
His eggs — to warm them in the sun:
Dear! what a hustle,
And bustle!
And there 's my aunt. I know her by her waist,
So long and thin,
And so pinched in,
Just in the pismire taste.
O! what are men? — Beings so small,
That, should I fall
Upon their little heads, I must
Crush them by hundreds into dust!
And what is life? and all its ages —
There 's seven stages!
Turnham Green! Chelsea! Putney! Fulham!
Brentford! and Kew!
And Tooting, too!
And O! what very little nags to pull 'em.
Yet each would seem a horse indeed,
If here at Paul's tip-top we 'd got 'em;
Although, like Cinderella's breed,
They 're mice at bottom.

Then let me not despise a horse,
Though he looks small from Paul's high-
cross!
Since he would be,— as near the sky,
— Fourteen hands high.
What is this world with London in its lap?
Mogg's Map.
The Thames, that ebbs and flows in its
broad channel?
A *tidy* kennel.
The bridges stretching from its banks?
Stone planks.
O me! hence could I read an admonition
To mad Ambition!
But that he would not listen to my call,
Though I should stand upon the cross, and
ball!

A VALENTINE.

O cruel heart! ere these posthumous papers
Have met thine eyes, I shall be out of breath;
Those cruel eyes, like two funereal tapers,
Have only lighted me the way to death.
Perchance, thou wilt extinguish them in vapors,
When I am gone, and green grass covereth
Thy lover, lost; but it will be in vain —
It will not bring the vital spark again.

Ah! when those eyes, like tapers, burned so blue,
  It seemed an omen that we must expect
The sprites of lovers: and it boded true,
  For I am half a sprite — a ghost elect;
Wherefore I write to thee this last adieu,
  With my last pen — before that I effect
My exit from the stage; just stopped before
The tombstone steps that lead us to death's door.

Full soon these living eyes, now liquid bright,
  Will turn dead dull, and wear no radiance, save
They shed a dreary and inhuman light,
  Illumed within by glow-worms of the grave;
These ruddy cheeks, so pleasant to the sight,
  These lusty legs, and all the limbs I have,
Will keep Death's carnival, and, foul or fresh,
Must bid farewell, a long farewell to flesh!

Yea, and this very heart, that dies for thee,
  As broken victuals to the worms will go;
And all the world will dine again but me —
  For I shall have no stomach; — and I know,
When I am ghostly, thou wilt sprightly be
  As now thou art: but will not tears of woe
Water thy spirits, with remorse adjunct,
When thou dost pause, and think of the defunct?

And when thy soul is buried in a sleep,
  In midnight solitude, and little dreaming
Of such a spectre — what if I should creep

Within thy presence in such dismal seeming?
Thine eyes will stare themselves awake, and weep,
And thou wilt cross thyself with treble screaming,
And pray with mingled penitence and dread
That I were less alive — or not so dead.

Then will thy heart confess thee, and reprove
This wilful homicide which thou hast done:
And the sad epitaph of so much love
Will eat into my heart, as if in stone:
And all the lovers that around thee move,
Will read my fate, and tremble for their own;
And strike upon their heartless breasts, and sigh,
"Man, born of woman, must of woman die!"

Mine eyes grow dropsical — I can no more —
And what is written thou may'st scorn to read,
Shutting thy tearless eyes.— 'Tis done — 'tis o'er —
My hand is destined for another deed.
But one last word wrung from its aching core,
And my lone heart in silentness will bleed;
Alas! it ought to take a life to tell
That one last word — that fare — fare — fare thee well!

A RECIPE — FOR CIVILIZATION.

THE following Poem — is from the pen of DOCTOR KITCHENER! — the most heterogeneous of authors, but at the same time — in the Sporting Latin of Mr. Egan — a real Homo-*genius*, or a Genius of a Man! In the Poem, his CULINARY ENTHUSIASM, as usual — ***boils over!*** and makes it seem written, as he describes himself (see the Cook's Oracle) — with the Spit in one hand! — and the Frying Pan in the other, — while in the style of the rhymes it is Hudibrastic,— as if in the ingredients of Versification, he had been assisted by his BUTLER!

As a Head Cook, Optician — Physician, Music Master — Domestic Economist and Death-bed Attorney! — I have celebrated The Author elsewhere with approbation; — and cannot now place him upon the Table *as a Poet*,— without still being his LAUDER, a phrase which those persons whose course of classical reading recalls the INFAMOUS FORGERY on *the Immortal Bard of Avon!* —— will find easy to understand.

SURELY, those sages err who teach
That man is known from brutes by speech,
Which hardly severs man from woman,
But not th' inhuman from the human —
Or else might parrots claim affinity,
And dogs be doctors by latinity,—
Not t' insist, (as might be shown,)
That beasts have gibberish of their own,
Which once was no dead tongue, tho' we
Since Esop's days have lost the key;

Nor yet to hint dumb men,— and, still, not
Beasts that could gossip though they will not,
But play at dummy like the monkeys,
For fear mankind should make them flunkies.
Neither can man be known by feature
Or form, because so like a creature,
That some grave men could never shape
Which is the aped and which the ape;
Nor by his gait, nor by his height,
Nor yet because he 's black or white,
But *rational*,— for so we call
The only COOKING ANIMAL!
The only one who brings his bit
Of dinner to the pot or spit,
For where 's the lion e'er was hasty,
To put his ven'son in a pasty?
Ergo, by logic, we repute,
That he who cooks is not a brute,—
But *Equus brutum est*, which means,
If a horse had sense he 'd boil his beans.
Nay, no one but a horse would forage
On naked oats instead of porridge;
Which proves, if brutes and Scotchmen vary,
The difference is culinary.
Further, as man is known by feeding
From brutes,— so men from men, in breeding
Are still distinguished as they eat,
And raw in manners, raw in meat,—
Look at the polished nations, hight
The civilized — the most polite

Is that which bears the praise of nations
For dressing eggs two hundred fashions;
Whereas, at savage feeders look,—
The less refined the less they cook;
From Tartar grooms that merely straddle
Across a steak and warm their saddle,
Down to the Abyssinian squaw,
That bolts her chops and collops raw,
And, like a wild beast, cares as little
To dress her person as her victual,—
For gowns, and gloves, and caps, and tippets,
Are beauty's sauces, spice, and sippets,
And not by shamble bodies put on,
But those who roast and boil their mutton;
So Eve and Adam wore no dresses
Because they lived on water-cresses,
And till they learned to cook their crudities,
Went blind as beetles to their nudities.
For niceness comes from th' inner side,
(As an ox is drest before his hide,)
And when the entrail loathes vulgarity
The outward man will soon cull rarity,
For 'tis th' effect of what we eat
To make a man look like his meat,
As insects show their food's complexions;
Thus fopling clothes are like confections.
But who, to feed a jaunty coxcomb,
Would have an Abyssinian ox come?
Or serve a dish of fricassees,
To clodpoles in a coat of frize?

Whereas a black would call for buffalo
Alive — and, no doubt, eat the offal too.
Now, (this premised,) it follows then
That certain culinary men
Should first go forth with pans and spits
To bring the heathens to their wits,
(For all wise Scotchmen of our century
Know that *first* steps are alimentary ; [pans
And, as we have proved, flesh pots and sauce-
Must pave the way for Wilberforce plans ;)
But Bunyan erred to think the near gate
To take man's soul, was battering Ear gate,
When reason should have worked her course
As men of war do — when their force
Can't take a town by open courage,
They steal an entry with its forage.
What reverend bishop, for example,
Could preach horned Apis from his temple ?
Whereas a cook would soon unseat him,
And make his own church-wardens eat him.
Not Irving could convert those vermin
The Anthropophages, by a sermon ;
Whereas your Osborne,* in a trice,
Would "take a shin of beef and spice," —
And raise them such a savoury smother,
No negro would devour his brother,
But turn his stomach round as loth
As Persians, to the old black broth,—

* Cook to the late Sir John Banks.

For knowledge oftenest makes an entry,
As well as true love, thro' the pantry,
Where beaux that came at first for feeding
Grow gallant men and get good breeding; —
Exempli gratia — in the West,
Ship-traders say there swims a nest
Lined with black natives, like a rookery,
But coarse as carrion crows at cookery.—
This race, though now called O. Y. E.* men,
(To show they are more than A. B. C. men,)
Was once so ignorant of our knacks
They laid their mats upon their backs,
And grew their quartern loaves for luncheon
On trees that baked them in the sunshine.
As for their bodies, they were coated,
(For painted things are so denoted;)
But, the naked truth is, stark primevals,
That said their prayers to timber devils,
Allowed polygamy — dwelt in wig-wams —
And, when they meant a feast, ate big yams.—
And why?— because their savage nook
Had ne'er been visited by Cook,—
And so they fared till our great chief,
Brought them, not Methodists, but beef
In tubs,— and taught them how to live,
Knowing it was too soon to give,
Just then, a homily on their sins,
(For cooking ends ere grace begins,)

* [Owhyee.]

Or hand his tracts to the untractable
Till they could keep a more exact table —
For nature has her proper courses,
And wild men must be backed like horses,
Which, jockeys know, are never fit
For riding till they 've had a bit
I' the mouth; but then, with proper tackle,
You may trot them to a tabernacle.
Ergo (I say) he first made changes
In the heathen modes, by kitchen ranges,
And taught the king's cook, by convincing
Process, that chewing was not mincing,
And in her black fist thrust a bundle
Of tracts abridged from Glasse and Rundell,
Where, ere she had read beyond Welsh rabbits,
She saw the spareness of her habits,
And round her loins put on a striped
Towel, where fingers might be wiped,
And then her breast clothed like her ribs,
(For aprons lead of course to bibs,)
And, by the time she had got a meat-
Screen, veiled her back, too, from the heat —
As for her gravies and her sauces,
(Tho' they reformed the royal fauces,)
Her forcemeats and ragouts,— I praise not,
Because the legend further says not,
Except, she kept each Christian high-day,
And once upon a fat good Fry-day
Ran short of logs, and told the Pagan,
That turned the spit, to chop up Dagon! —

"PLEASE TO RING THE BELLE."

I.

I 'LL tell you a story that 's not in Tom Moore: —
Young Love likes to knock at a pretty girl's door:
So he called upon Lucy — 'twas just ten o'clock —
Like a spruce single man, with a smart double
knock.

II.

Now a hand-maid, whatever her fingers be at,
Will run like a puss when she hears a *rat*-tat:
So Lucy ran up — and in two seconds more
Had questioned the stranger and answered the
door.

III.

The meeting was bliss; but the parting was woe:
For the moment will come when such comers
must go;
So she kissed him, and whispered — poor inno-
cent thing —
"The next time you come, love, pray come with
a ring."

THE MERMAID OF MARGATE.

> "Alas! what perils do environ
> That man who meddles with a siren!"
>
> HUDIBRAS.

ON Margate beach, where the sick one roams,
And the sentimental reads;
Where the maiden flirts, and the widow comes —
Like the ocean — to cast her weeds; —

Where urchins wander to pick up shells,
And the Cit to spy at the ships,—
Like the water gala at Sadler's Wells,—
And the Chandler for watery dips; —

There's a maiden sits by the ocean brim,
As lovely and fair as sin!
But woe, deep water and woe to him,
That she snareth like Peter Fin!

Her head is crowned with pretty sea-wares,
And her locks are golden and loose:
And seek to her feet, like other folks' heirs,
To stand, of course, in her shoes!

And, all day long, she combeth them well,
With a sea-shark's prickly jaw;
And her mouth is just like a rose-lipped shell,
The fairest that man e'er saw!

And the Fishmonger, humble as love may be,
Hath planted his seat by her side;
"Good even, fair maid! Is thy lover at sea,
To make thee so watch the tide?"

She turned about with her pearly brows,
And clasped him by the hand;
"Come, love, with me; I 've a bonny house
On the golden Goodwin Sand."

And then she gave him a siren kiss,
No honeycomb e'er was sweeter:
Poor wretch! how little he dreamt for this
That Peter should be salt-Peter:

And away with her prize to the wave she leapt,
Not walking, as damsels do,
With toe and heel, as she ought to have stept,
But she hopt like a Kangaroo;

One plunge, and then the victim was blind,
Whilst they galloped across the tide;
At last, on the bank he waked in his mind,
And the beauty was by his side.

One half on the sand, and half in the sea,
  But his hair all began to stiffen ;
For when he looked where her feet should be,
  She had no more feet than Miss Biffen !

But a scaly tail, of a dolphin's growth,
  In the dabbling brine did soak :
At last she opened her pearly mouth,
  Like an oyster, and thus she spoke :

" You crimpt my father, who was a skate ; —
  And my sister you sold — a maid ;
So here remain for a fishery fate,
  For lost you are, and betrayed ! "

And away she went, with a sea-gull's scream,
  And a splash of her saucy tail ;
In a moment he lost the silvery gleam
  That shone on her splendid mail !

The sun went down with a blood-red flame,
  And the sky grew cloudy and black,
And the tumbling billows like leap-frog came,
  Each over the other's back !

Ah, me ! it had been a beautiful scene,
  With the safe *terra-firma* round ;
But the green water hillocks all seemed to him,
  Like those in a churchyard ground ;

And Christians love in the turf to lie,
Not in watery graves to be ;
Nay, the very fishes will sooner die
On the land than in the sea.

And whilst he stood, the watery strife
Encroached on every hand,
And the ground decreased — his moments of life
Seemed measured, like Time's, by sand ;

And still the waters foamed in, like ale,
In front, and on either flank,
He knew that Goodwin and Co. must fail,
There was such a run on the bank.

A little more, and a little more,
The surges came tumbling in ;
He sang the evening hymn twice o'er,
And thought of every sin !

Each flounder and plaice lay cold at his heart,
As cold as his marble slab ;
And he thought he felt in every part,
The pincers of scalded crab.

The squealing lobsters that he had boiled,
And the little potted shrimps,
All the horny prawns he had ever spoiled,
Gnawed into his soul, like imps !

And the billows were wandering to and fro,
  And the glorious sun was sunk,
And Day, getting black in the face, as though
  Of the nightshade she had drunk !

Had there been but a smuggler's cargo adrift,
  One tub, or keg, to be seen ;
It might have given his spirits a lift
  Or an *anker* where *Hope* might lean !

But there was not a box or a beam afloat,
  To raft him from that sad place ;
Not a skiff, nor a yawl, or a mackerel boat,
  Nor a smack upon Neptune's face.

At last, his lingering hopes to buoy,
  He saw a sail and a mast,
And called " Ahoy ! "— but it was not a hoy,
  And so the vessel went past.

And with saucy wing that flapped in his face,
  The wild bird about him flew,
With a shrilly scream, that twitted his case,
  " Why, thou art a sea-gull too ! "

And lo ! the tide was over his feet ;
  O ! his heart began to freeze,
And slowly to pulse : — in another beat
  The wave was up to his knees !

He was deafened amidst the mountain tops,
  And the salt spray blinded his eyes,
And washed away the other salt drops
  That grief had caused to arise: —

But just as his body was all afloat,
  And the surges above him broke,
He was saved from the hungry deep by a boat
  Of Deal — (but builded of oak.)

The skipper gave him a dram, as he lay,
  And chafed his shivering skin;
And the Angel returned that was flying away
  With the spirit of Peter Fin!

THE LADY AT SEA.

Cables entangling her,
Shipspars for mangling her,
Ropes, sure of strangling her;
Blocks over-dangling her;
Tiller to batter her,
Topmast to shatter her,
Tobacco to spatter her;
Boreas blustering,
Boatswain quite flustering,
Thunder-clouds mustering

To blast her with sulphur —
If the deep don't ingulph her;
Sometimes fear's scrutiny
Pries out a mutiny,
Sniffs conflagration,
Or hints at starvation: —
All the sea dangers,
Buccaneers, rangers,
Pirates, and Sallee-men,
Algerine galleymen,
Tornadoes and typhons,
And horrible siphons,
And submarine travels
Thro' roaring sea-navels;
Every thing wrong enough,
Long-boat not long enough,
Vessel not strong enough;
Pitch marring frippery,
The deck very slippery,
And the cabin — built sloping,
The Captain a-toping,
And the Mate a blasphemer,
That names his Redeemer —
With inward uneasiness;
The cook, known by greasiness,
The victuals beslubbered,
Her bed — in a cupboard;
Things of strange christening,
Snatched in her listening,
Blue lights and red lights,

And mention of dead lights,
And shrouds made a theme of,
Things horrid to dream of,—
And *buoys* in the water
To fear all exhort her:
Her friend no Leander;
Herself no sea gander,
And ne'er a cork jacket
On board of the packet;
The breeze still a-stiffening,
The trumpet quite deafening;
Thoughts of repentance,
And doomsday and sentence;
Every thing sinister,
Not a church minister,—
Pilot a blunderer,
Coral reefs under her,
Ready to sunder her;
Trunks tipsy-topsy,
The ship in a dropsy;
Waves oversurging her,
Sirens a dirgeing her,
Sharks all expecting her,
Sword-fish dissecting her,
Crabs with their hand-vices
Punishing land vices;
Sea-dogs and unicorns,
Things with no puny horns,
Mermen carnivorous —
"Good Lord deliver us!"

THE STAG-EYED LADY.

A MOORISH TALE.

Schehera ade immediately began the following story.

ALI BEN ALI (did you never read
His wondrous acts that chronicles relate,—
How there was one in pity might exceed
The sack of Troy?) Magnificent he sate
Upon the throne of greatness — great indeed,
For those that he had under him were great —
The horse he rode on, shod with silver nails,
Was a Bashaw — Bashaws have horses' tails.

Ali was cruel — a most cruel one!
'Tis rumoured he had strangled his own mother —
Howbeit such deeds of darkness he had done,
'Tis thought he would have slain his elder brother
And sister too — but happily that none
Did live within *harms* length of one another,
Else he had sent the Sun in all its blaze
To endless night, and shortened the Moon's days.

Despotic power, that mars a weak man's wit,
And makes a bad man — absolutely bad,
Made Ali wicked — to a fault: —'tis fit
Monarchs should have some check-strings; but he had
No curb upon his will — no, not a *bit* —
Wherefore he did not reign well — and full glad
His slaves had been to hang him — but they faltered,
And let him live unhanged — and still unaltered.

Until he got a sage bush of a beard,
Wherein an Attic owl might roost — a trail
Of bristly hair — that, honoured and unsheared,
Grew downward like old women and cow's tail:
Being a sign of age — some gray appeared,
Mingling with duskier brown its warnings pale;
But yet not so poetic as when Time
Comes like Jack Frost, and whitens it in rime.

Ben Ali took the hint, and much did vex
His royal bosom that he had no son,
No living child of the more noble sex,
To stand in his Morocco shoes — not one
To make a negro-pollard — or tread necks
When he was gone — doomed, when his days were done,
To leave the very city of his fame
Without an Ali to keep up his name.

Therefore he chose a lady for his love,
  Singling from out the herd one stag-eyed dear;
So called, because her lustrous eyes, above
  All eyes, were dark, and timorous, and clear;
Then through his Muftis piously he strove,
  And drummed with proxy-prayers Mohammed's
    ear,
Knowing a boy for certain must come out of it,
Or else he was not praying to his *Profit.*

Beer will grow *mothery*, and ladies fair [dame:
  Will grow like beer; so did that stag-eyed
Ben Ali, hoping for a son and heir,
  Boyed up his hopes, and even chose a name
Of mighty hero that his child should bear;
  He made so certain ere his chicken came:
But oh! all worldly wit is little worth,
Nor knoweth what to-morrow will bring forth.

To-morrow came, and with to-morrow's sun
  A little daughter to this world of sins,
Miss-fortunes never come alone — so one
  Brought on another, like a pair of twins:
Twins! female twins! — it was enough to stun
  Their little wits and scare them from their skins,
To hear their father stamp, and curse and swear,
Pulling his beard because he had no heir.

Then strove their stag-eyed mother to calm down
  This his parental rage, and thus addrest:

"O! Most Serene! why dost thou stamp and
frown,
And box the compass of the royal chest?
Ah! thou wilt mar that portly trunk, I own
I love to gaze on! — Pr'ythee, thou hadst best
Pocket thy fists. Nay, love, if you so thin
Your beard, you'll want a wig upon your chin!"

But not her words, or even her tears, could slack
The quicklime of his rage, that hotter grew:
He called his slaves to bring an ample sack
Wherein a woman might be *poked* — a few
Dark grimly men felt pity and looked black
At this sad order; but their slaveships knew
When any dared demur, his sword so bending
Cut off the "head and front of their offending."

For Ali had a sword, much like himself,
A crooked blade, guilty of human gore —
The trophies it had lopped from many an elf
Were stuck at his *head*-quarters by the score —
Nor yet in peace he laid it on the shelf,
But jested with it, and his wit cut sore;
So that (as they of Public Houses speak)
He often did his dozen *butts* a week.

Therefore his slaves, with most obedient fears,
Came with the sack the lady to inclose;
In vain from her stag-eyes "the big round tears
Coursed one another down her innocent nose;"

In vain her tongue wept sorrow in their ears;
Though there were some felt willing to oppose,
Yet when their heads came in their heads, that minute,
Though 'twas a piteous *case*, they put her in it.

And when the sack was tied, some two or three
Of these black undertakers slowly brought her
To a kind of Moorish Serpentine; for she
Was doomed to have *a winding-sheet of water*.
Then farewell, earth — farewell to the green tree —
Farewell, the sun — the moon — each little daughter!
She 's shot from off the shoulders of a black,
Like a bag of Wall's-End from a coalman's back.

The waters oped, and the wide sack full-filled
All that the waters oped, as down it fell;
Then closed the wave, and then the surface rilled
A ring above her, like a water-knell;
A moment more, and all its face was stilled,
And not a guilty heave was left to tell
That underneath its calm and blue transparence
A dame lay drowned in her sack, like Clarence.

But Heaven beheld, and awful witness bore,
The moon in black eclipse deceased that night,
Like Desdemona smothered by the Moor
The lady's natal star with pale affright

Fainted and fell — and what were stars before,
Turned comets as the tale was brought to light;
And all looked downward on the fatal wave,
And made their own reflections on her grave.

Next night, a head — a little lady head,
Pushed through the waters a most glassy face,
With weedy tresses, thrown apart and spread,
Combed by 'live ivory, to show the space
Of a pale forehead, and two eyes that shed
A soft blue mist, breathing a bloomy grace
Over their sleepy lids — and so she raised
Her *aqua*line nose above the stream, and gazed.

She oped her lips — lips of a gentle blush,
So pale it seemed near drowned to a white,—
She oped her lips, and forth there sprang a gush
Of music bubbling through the surface light;
The leaves are motionless, the breezes hush
To listen to the air — and through the night
There come these words of a most plaintive ditty,
Sobbing as they would break all hearts with pity:

THE WATER PERI'S SONG.

Farewell, farewell, to my mother's own daughter,
The child that she wet-nursed is lapped in the wave

The *Mussul*man coming to fish in this water,
Adds a tear to the flood that weeps over her grave.

This sack is her coffin, this water 's her bier,
This grayish *bath* cloak is her funeral pall,
And, stranger, O stranger! this song that you hear
Is her epitaph, elegy, dirges, and all!

Farewell, farewell, to the child of Al Hassan,
My mother's own daughter — the last of her race —
She 's a corpse, the poor body! and lies in this basin,
And sleeps in the water that washes her face.

A LEGEND OF NAVARRE.

I.

'Twas in the reign of Lewis, called the Great,
As one may read on his triumphal arches,
The thing befell I'm going to relate,
In course of one of those "pomposo" marches
He loved to make, like any gorgeous Persian,
Partly for war, and partly for diversion.

II.

Some wag had put it in the royal brain
  To drop a visit at an old chateau,
Quite unexpected, with his courtly train;
  The monarch liked it,— but it happened so,
That Death had got before them by a post,
And they were "reckoning without their *host*,"

III.

Who died exactly as a child should die,
  Without one groan or a convulsive breath,
Closing without one pang his quiet eye,
  Sliding composedly from sleep — to death;
A corpse so placid ne'er adorned a bed,
He seemed not quite — but only rather dead.

IV.

All night the widowed Baroness contrived
  To shed a widow's tears; but on the morrow
Some news of such unusual sort arrived,
  There came strange alteration in her sorrow;
From mouth to mouth it passed, one common humming
Throughout the house — the King! the King is coming!

V.

The Baroness, with all her soul and heart,
  A loyal woman, (now called ultra royal,)
Soon thrust all funeral concerns apart,
  And only thought about a banquet royal;

In short, by aid of earnest preparation,
The visit quite dismissed the visitation.

VI.

And, spite of all her grief for the ex-mate,
There was a secret hope she could not smother,
That some one, early, might replace "the late"—
It was too soon to think about another;
Yet let her minutes of despair be reckoned
Against her hope, which was but for *a second.*

VII.

She almost thought that being thus bereft
Just then, was one of time's propitious touches;
A thread in such a nick so nicked, it left
Free opportunity to be a duchess;
Thus all her care was only to look pleasant,
But as for tears — she dropped them — for the present.

VIII.

Her household, as good servants ought to try,
Looked like their lady — any thing but sad,
And giggled even that they might not cry,
To damp fine company; in truth they had
No time to mourn, through choking turkeys' throttles,
Scouring old laces, and reviewing bottles.

IX.

O what a hubbub for the house of woe!
All, resolute to one irresolution,
Kept tearing, swearing, plunging to and fro,
Just like another French mob-revolution.
There lay the corpse that could not stir a muscle,
But all the rest seemed Chaos in a bustle.

X.

The Monarch came: O! who could ever guess
The Baroness had been so late a weeper!
The kingly grace and more than graciousness,
Buried the poor defunct some fathoms deep-
er,—
Could he have had a glance — alas, poor Being!
Seeing would certainly have led to *D*—ing.

XI.

For casting round about her eyes to find
Some one to whom her chattels to indorse,
The comfortable dame at last inclined
To choose the cheerful Master of the Horse;
He was so gay,— so tender,— the complete
Nice man,— the sweetest of the monarch's suite.

XII.

He saw at once and entered in the lists —
Glance unto glance made amorous replies;
They talked together like two egotists,
In conversation all made up of *eyes:*

No couple ever got so right consort-ish
Within two hours — a courtship rather shortish.

XIII.

At last, some sleepy, some by wine opprest,
  The courtly company began "nid noddin;"
The King first sought his chamber, and the rest
  Instanter followed by the course he trod in.
I shall not please the scandalous by showing
The order, or disorder of their going.

XIV

The old Chateau, before that night, had never
  Held half so many underneath its roof;
It tasked the Baroness's best endeavour,
  And put her best contrivance to the proof,
To give them chambers up and down the stairs,
In twos and threes, by singles, and by pairs.

XV.

She had just lodging for the whole — yet barely;
  And some, that were both broad of back and tall,
Lay on spare beds that served them very sparely;
  However, there were beds enough for all;
But living bodies occupied so many,
She could not let the dead one take up any!

XVI.

The act was, certainly, not over decent: [him,
  Some small respect, e'en after death, she owed

Considering his death had been so recent;
 However, by command, her servants stowed
 him,
(I am ashamed to think how he was slubbered,)
Stuck bolt upright within a corner cupboard!

XVII.

And there he slept as soundly as a post,
 With no more pillow than an oaken shelf;
Just like a kind accommodating host,
 Taking all inconvenience on himself;
None else slept in that room, except a stranger,
A decent man, a sort of Forest Ranger.

XVIII.

Who, whether he had gone too soon to bed,
 Or dreamt himself into an appetite,
Howbeit, he took a longing to be fed,
 About the hungry middle of the night;
So getting forth, he sought some scrap to eat,
Hopeful of some stray pasty, or cold meat.

XIX.

The casual glances of the midnight moon,
 Brightening some antique ornaments of brass,
Guided his gropings to that corner soon,
 Just where it stood, the coffin-safe, alas!
He tried the door — then shook it — and in
 course
Of time it opened to a little force.

XX.

He put one hand in, and began to grope ;
  The place was very deep, and quite as dark as
The middle night ; — when lo ! beyond his hope,
  He felt a something cold,—in fact, the carcase ;
Right overjoyed, he laughed, and blest his luck
At finding, as he thought, this haunch of buck !

XXI.

Then striding back for his couteau de chasse,
  Determined on a little midnight lunching,
He came again and probed about the mass,
  As if to find the fattest bit for munching ;
Not meaning wastefully to cut it all up,
But only to abstract a little collop.

XXII.

But just as he had struck one greedy stroke,
  His hand fell down quite powerless and weak ;
For when he cut the haunch it plainly spoke
  As haunch of venison never ought to speak ;
No wonder that his hand could go no further —
Whose could ? — to carve cold meat that bellowed,
    " murther ! "

XXIII.

Down came the Body with a bounce, and down
  The Ranger sprang, a staircase at a spring,
And bawled enough to waken up a town ;

Some thought that *they* were murdered, some,
the King,
And, like Macduff, did nothing for a season,
But stand upon the spot and bellow, "Treason!"

XXIV.

A hundred nightcaps gathered in a mob,
Torches drew torches, swords brought swords
together,
It seemed so dark and perilous a job;
The Baroness came trembling like a feather
Just in the rear, as pallid as a corse,
Leaning against the Master of the Horse.

XXV.

A dozen of the bravest up the stair, [ber;
Well lighted and well watched, began to clam-
They sought the door — they found it — they
were there,
A dozen heads went poking in the chamber;
And lo! with one hand planted on his hurt,
There stood the Body bleeding thro' his shirt,—

XXVI.

No passive corse — but like a duellist
Just smarting from a scratch — in fierce position,
One hand advanced, and ready to resist;
In fact, the Baron doffed the apparition,
Swearing those oaths the French delight in most,
And for the second time "gave up the ghost!"

XXVII.

A living miracle ! — for why ? — the knife
  That cuts so many off from grave gray hairs,
Had only carved him kindly into life :
  How soon it changed the posture of affairs !
The difference one person more or less
Will make in families, is past all guess.

XXVIII.

There stood the Baroness — no widow yet :
  Here stood the Baron — " in the body " still :
There stood the Horses' Master in a pet,
  Choking with disappointment's bitter pill,
To see the hope of his reversion fail,
Like that of riding on a donkey's tail.

XXIX.

The Baron lived — 'twas nothing but a trance :
  The lady died — 'twas nothing but a death :
The cupboard-cut served only to enhance
  This postscript to the old Baronial breath : —
He soon forgave, for the revival's sake,
A little *chop* intended for a *steak !*

A TRUE STORY.

Of all our pains, since man was curst,
I mean of body, not the mental,
To name the worst, among the worst,
The dental sure is transcendental;
Some bit of masticating bone,
That ought to help to clear a shelf,
But let its proper work alone,
And only seems to gnaw itself;
In fact, of any grave attack
On victuals there is little danger,
'Tis so like coming to the *rack*,
As well as going to the manger.

Old Hunks — it seemed a fit retort
Of justice on his grinding ways —
Possessed a grinder of the sort,
That troubled all his latter days.
The best of friends fall out, and so
His teeth had done some years ago,
Save some old stumps with ragged root,
And they took turn about to shoot;
If he drank any chilly liquor,
They made it quite a point to throb;
But if he warmed it on the hob,
Why then they only twitched the quicker.

One tooth — I wonder such a tooth
Had never killed him in his youth —
One tooth he had with many fangs,
That shot at once as many pangs,
It had an universal sting;
One touch of that extatic stump
Could jerk his limbs, and make him jump,
Just like a puppet on a string;
And what was worse than all, it had
A way of making others bad.
There is, as many know, a knack,
With certain farming undertakers,
And this same tooth pursued their track,
By adding *achers* still to *achers!*

One way there is, that has been judged
A certain cure, but Hunks was loth
To pay the fee, and quite begrudged
To lose his tooth and money both;
In fact, a dentist and the wheel
Of Fortune are a kindred cast,
For after all is drawn, you feel
Its paying for a blank at last;
So Hunks went on from week to week,
And kept his torment in his cheek;
Oh! how it sometimes set him rocking,
With that perpetual gnaw — gnaw — gnaw,
His moans and groans were truly shocking
And loud — altho' he held his jaw.
Many a tug he gave his gum,
And tooth, but still it would not come,

Tho' tied by string to some firm thing,
He could not draw it, do his best,
By drawers, altho' he tried a chest.

At last, but after much debating,
He joined a score of mouths in waiting,
Like his, to have their troubles out.
Sad sight it was to look about
At twenty faces making faces,
With many a rampant trick and antic,
For all were very horrid cases,
And made their owners nearly frantic.
A little wicket now and then
Took one of these unhappy men,
And out again the victim rushed,
While eyes and mouth together gushed ;
At last arrived our hero's turn,
Who plunged his hands in both his pockets,
And down he sat prepared to learn
How teeth are charmed to quit their sockets.

Those who have felt such operations,
Alone can guess the sort of ache,
When his old tooth began to break
The thread of old associations ;
It touched a string in every part,
It had so many tender ties ;
One chord seemed wrenching at his heart,
And two were tugging at his eyes ;
" Bone of his bone," he felt of course,
As husbands do in such divorce ;

At last the fangs gave way a little,
Hunks gave his head a backward jerk,
And lo! the cause of all this work,
Went — where it used to send his victual!
The monstrous pain of this proceeding
Had not so numbed his miser wit,
But in this slip he saw a hit
To save, at least, his purse from bleeding;
So when the dentist sought his fees,
Quoth Hunks, "Let's finish, if you please."
"How, finish! why it's out!" — "Oh! no —
I'm none of your beforehand tippers,
'Tis you are out, to argue so;
My tooth is in my head no doubt,
But as you say you pulled it out,
Of course it's there — between your nippers."
"Zounds! sir, d'ye think I'd sell the truth
To get a fee? no, wretch, I scorn it."
But Hunks still asked to see the tooth,
And swore by gum! he had not drawn it.
His end obtained, he took his leave,
A secret chuckle in his sleeve;
The joke was worthy to produce one,
To think, by favour of his wit,
How well a dentist had been bit
By one old stump, and that a loose one!

The thing was worth a laugh, but mirth
Is still the frailest thing on earth:
Alas! how often when a joke

Seems in our sleeve, and safe enough,
There comes some unexpected stroke,
And hangs a weeper on the cuff!
Hunks had not whistled half a mile,
When, planted right against a stile,
There stood his foeman, Mike Mahoney,
A vagrant reaper, Irish-born,
That helped to reap our miser's corn,
But had not helped to reap his money,
A fact that Hunks remembered quickly;
His whistle all at once was quelled,
And when he saw how Michael held
His sickle, he felt rather sickly.

Nine souls in ten, with half his fright,
Would soon have paid the bill at sight,
But misers (let observers watch it)
Will never part with their delight
Till well demanded by a hatchet —
They live hard — and they die to match it.
Thus Hunks prepared for Mike's attacking,
Resolved not yet to pay the debt,
But let him take it out in hacking;
However, Mike began to stickle
In word before he used the sickle;
But mercy was not long attendant:
From words at last he took to blows
And aimed a cut at Hunks's nose;
That made it what some folks are not —
A member very independent.

Heaven knows how far this cruel trick
Might still have led, but for a tramper
That came in danger's very nick,
To put Mahoney to the scamper.
But still compassion met a damper;
There lay the severed nose, alas!
Beside the daisies on the grass,
"Wee, crimson-tipt" as well as they,
According to the poet's lay:
And there stood Hunks, no sight for laughter!
Away ran Hodge to get assistance,
With nose in hand, which Hunks ran after,
But somewhat at unusual distance.
In many a little country place
It is a very common case
To have but one residing doctor,
Whose practice rather seems to be
No practice, but a rule of three,
Physician — surgeon — drug-decocter;
Thus Hunks was forced to gô once more
Where he had ta'en his tooth before.
His mere name made the learned man hot,—
"What! Hunks again within my door!
I'll pull his nose;" quoth Hunks, "You cannot."

The doctor looked and saw the case
Plain as the nose *not* on his face.
"O! hum — ha — yes — I understand."
But then arose a long demur,

For not a finger would he stir
Till he was paid his fee in hand;
That matter settled, there they were,
With Hunks well strapped upon his chair.

The opening of a surgeon's job —
His tools, a chestful or a drawerful —
Are always something very awful,
And give the heart the strangest throb;
But never patient in his funks
Looked half so like a ghost as Hunks,
Or surgeon half so like a devil
Prepared for some infernal revel:
His huge black eye kept rolling, rolling,
Just like a bolus in a box,
His fury seemed above controlling,
He bellowed like a hunted ox:
"Now, swindling wretch, I'll show thee how
We treat such cheating knaves as thou;
Oh! sweet is this revenge to sup;
I have thee by the nose — it's now
My turn — and I will turn it up."

Guess how the miser liked this scurvy
And cruel way of venting passion;
The snubbing folks in this new fashion
Seemed quite to turn him topsy turvy;
He uttered prayers, and groans, and curses,
For things had often gone amiss
And wrong with him before, but this

Would be the worst of all *reverses!*
In fancy he beheld his snout
Turned upward like a pitcher's spout;
There was another grievance yet,
And fancy did not fail to show it,
That he must throw a summerset,
Or stand upon his head to blow it.
And was there then no argument
To change the doctor's vile intent,
And move his pity? — yes, in truth,
And that was — paying for the tooth.
"Zounds! pay for such a stump! I 'd rather —
But here the menace went no farther,
For with his other ways of pinching,
Hunks had a miser's love of snuff,
A recollection strong enough
To cause a very serious flinching;
In short, he paid, and had the feature
Replaced as it was meant by nature;
For tho' by this 'twas cold to handle,
(No corpse's could have felt more horrid,)
And white just like an end of candle,
The doctor deemed and proved it too,
That noses from the nose will do
As well as noses from the forehead;
So, fixed by dint of rag and lint,
The part was bandaged up and muffled.
The chair unfastened, Hunks arose,
And shuffled out, for once unshuffled;
And as he went these words he snuffled —
"Well, this *is* 'paying through the nose.'"

THE MONKEY-MARTYR.

A FABLE.

"God help thee, said I, but I'll let thee out, cost what it will; so I turned about the cage to get to the door."

STERNE.

'Tis strange, what awkward figures and odd capers
Folks cut, who seek their doctrine from the papers;
But there are many shallow politicians
Who take their bias from bewildered journals —
Turn state-physicians,
And make themselves fools'-caps of the diurnals.

One of this kind, not human, but a monkey,
Had read himself at last to this sour creed —
That he was nothing but Oppression's flunkey,
And man a tyrant over all his breed.
He could not read
Of niggers whipt, or over-trampled weavers,
But he applied their wrongs to his own seed,
And nourished thoughts that threw him into fevers.
His very dreams were full of martial beavers,
And drilling Pugs, for liberty pugnacious,
To sever chains vexatious:

In fact, he thought that all his injured line
Should take up pikes in hand, and never drop 'em
Till they had cleared a road to Freedom's shrine,—
Unless perchance the turnpike men should stop 'em.

Full of this rancour,
Pacing one day beside St. Clement Danes
It came into his brains
To give a look in at the Crown and Anchor;
Where certain solemn sages of the nation
Were at that moment in deliberation
How to relieve the wide world of its chains,
Pluck despots down,
And thereby crown
Whitee- as well as blackee-man-cipation.
Pug heard the speeches with great approbation,
And gazed with pride upon the Liberators;
To see mere coal-heavers
Such perfect Bolivars —
Waiters of inns sublimed to innovators,
And slaters dignified as legislators —
Small publicans demanding (such their high sense
Of liberty) an universal license —
And pattern-makers easing Freedom's clogs —
The whole thing seemed
So fine, he deemed
The smallest demagogues as great as Gogs!

Pug, with some curious notions in his noddle,
Walked out at last, and turned into the Strand,
To the left hand,
Conning some portion of the previous twaddle,
And striding with a step that seemed designed
To represent the mighty March of Mind,
Instead of that slow waddle
Of thought, to which our ancestors inclined —
No wonder, then, that he should quickly find
He stood in front of that intrusive pile,
Where Cross keeps many a kind
Of bird confined,
And free-born animal, in durance vile —
A thought that stirred up all the monkey-bile!

The window stood ajar —
It was not far,
Nor, like Parnassus, very hard to climb —
The hour was verging on the supper-time,
And many a growl was sent through many a bar.
Meanwhile Pug scrambled upward like a tar,
And soon crept in,
Unnoticed in the din
Of tuneless throats, that made the attics ring
With all the harshest notes that they could bring;
For like the Jews,
Wild beasts refuse
In midst of their captivity — to sing.

Lord! how it made him chafe,
Full of his new emancipating zeal,
To look around upon this brute-bastile,
And see the king of creatures in — a safe!
The desert's denizen in one small den,
Swallowing slavery's most bitter pills —
A bear in bars unbearable. And then
The fretful porcupine, with all its quills,
Imprisoned in a pen!
A tiger limited to four feet ten;
And, still worse lot,
A leopard to one spot,
An elephant enlarged,
But not discharged;
(It was before the elephant was shot;)
A doleful wanderow, that wandered not;
An ounce much disproportioned to his pound.
Pug's wrath waxed hot
To gaze upon these captive creatures round;
Whose claws — all scratching — gave him full assurance
They found their durance vile of vile endurance.

He went above — a solitary mounter
Up gloomy stairs — and saw a pensive group
Of hapless fowls —
Cranes, vultures, owls,
In fact, it was a sort of Poultry-Compter,
Where feathered prisoners were doomed to droop:
Here sat an eagle, forced to make a stoop,

Not from the skies, but his impending roof;
And there aloof,
A pining ostrich, moping in a coop;
With other samples of the bird creation,
All caged against their powers and their wills,
And cramped in such a space, the longest bills
Were plainly bills of least accommodation.
In truth, it was a very ugly scene
To fall to any liberator's share,
To see those winged fowls, that once had been
Free as the wind, no freer than fixed air.

His temper little mended,
Pug from this Bird-cage Walk at last descended
Unto the lion and the elephant,
His bosom in a pant
To see all nature's Free List thus suspended,
And beasts deprived of what she had intended.
They could not even prey
In their own way;
A hardship always reckoned quite prodigious.
Thus he revolved —
And soon resolved
To give them freedom, civil and religious.

That night, there were no country cousins, raw
From Wales to view the lion and his kin:
The keeper's eyes were fixed upon a saw;
The saw was fixed upon a bullock's shin.
Meanwhile with stealthy paw,

Pug hastened to withdraw
The bolt that kept the king of brutes within.
Now, monarch of the forest! thou shalt win
Precious enfranchisement — thy bolts are undone;
Thou art no longer a degraded creature,
But loose to roam with liberty and nature;
And free of all the jungles about London —
All Hampstead's heathy desert lies before thee!
Methinks I see thee bound from Cross's ark,
Full of the native instinct that comes o'er thee,
And turn a ranger
Of Hounslow Forest, and the Regent's Park —
Thin Rhodes's cows — the mail-coach steeds endanger —
And gobble parish watchmen after dark: —
Methinks I see thee, with the early lark,
Stealing to Merlin's cave — (*thy* cave) — Alas,
That such bright visions should not come to pass!
Alas for freedom, and for freedom's hero!
Alas, for liberty of life and limb!
For Pug had only half unbolted Nero,
When Nero *bolted him!*

CRANIOLOGY.

'Tis strange how like a very dunce,
Man — with his bumps upon his sconce,
Has lived so long, and yet no knowledge he
Has had, till lately, of Phrenology —
A science that by simple dint of
Head-combing he should find a hint of,
When scratching o'er those little poll-hills,
The faculties throw up like mole-hills; —
A science that, in very spite
Of all his teeth, ne'er came to light,
For tho' he knew his skull had *grinders*,
Still there turned up no *organ* finders,
Still sages wrote, and ages fled,
And no man's head came in his head —
Not even the pate of Erra Pater,
Knew aught about its pia mater.
At last great Dr. Gall bestirs him —
I don't know but it might be Spurzheim —
Tho' native of a dull and slow land,
And makes partition of our Poll-land;
At our Acquisitiveness guesses,
And all those necessary *nesses*
Indicative of human habits,
All burrowing in the head like rabbits.

Thus Veneration, he made known,
Had got a lodging at the Crown:
And Music (see Deville's example)
A set of chambers in the Temple:
That Language taught the tongues close by
And took in pupils thro' the eye,
Close by his neighbour Computation,
Who taught the eyebrows numeration.

The science thus — to speak in fit
Terms — having struggled from its nit,
Was seized on by a swarm of Scotchmen,
Those scientifical hotch-potch men,
Who have at least a penny dip
And wallop in all doctorship,
Just as in making broth they smatter
By bobbing twenty things in water:
These men, I say, made quick appliance
And close, to phrenologic science:
For of all learned themes whatever
That schools and colleges deliver,
There 's none they love so near the bodles,
As analyzing their own noddles,
Thus in a trice each northern blockhead
Had got his fingers in his shock head,
And of his bumps was babbling yet worse
Than poor Miss Capulet's dry wet-nurse;
Till having been sufficient rangers
Of their own heads, they took to strangers'
And found in Presbyterians' polls
The things they hated in their souls;

For Presbyterians hear with passion
Of organs joined with veneration.
No kind there was of human pumpkin
But at its bumps it had a bumpkin;
Down to the very lowest gullion,
And oiliest scull of oily scullion,
No great man died but this they *did* do,
They begged his cranium of his widow:
No murderer died by law disaster,
But they took off his sconce in plaster;
For thereon they could show depending,
"The head and front of his offending,"
How that his philanthropic bump
Was mastered by a baser lump;
For every bump (these wags insist)
Has its direct antagonist,
Each striving stoutly to prevail,
Like horses knotted tail to tail;
And many a stiff and sturdy battle
Occurs between these adverse cattle,
The secret cause, beyond all question,
Of aches ascribed to indigestion,—
Whereas 'tis but two knobby rivals
Tugging together like sheer devils,
Till one gets mastery good or sinister,
And comes in like a new prime-minister.

Each bias in some master node is:—
What takes M'Adam where a road is,
To hammer little pebbles less?
His organ of Destructiveness.

What makes great Joseph so encumber
Debate? a lumping lump of Number:
Or Malthus rail at babies so?
The smallness of his Philopro —
What severs man and wife? a simple
Defect of the Adhesive pimple:
Or makes weak women go astray?
Their bumps are more in fault than they.
These facts being found and set in order
By grave M. D.'s beyond the Border,
To make them for some few months eternal,
Were entered monthly in a journal,
That many a northern sage still writes in,
And throws his little Northern Lights in,
And proves and proves about the phrenos,
A great deal more than I or he knows.
How Music suffers, *par exemple*,
By wearing tight hats round the temple;
What ills great boxers have to fear
From blisters put behind the ear:
And how a porter's Veneration
Is hurt by porter's occupation:
Whether shillelahs in reality
May deaden Individuality:
Or tongs and poker be creative
Of alterations in the Amative:
If falls from scaffolds make us less
Inclined to all Constructiveness:
With more such matters, all applying
To heads — and therefore *head*ifying.

A PARTHIAN GLANCE.

"Sweet Memory, wafted by thy gentle gale,
Oft up the stream of time I turn my sail."
ROGERS.

COME, my Crony, let's think upon far-away days,
And lift up a little Oblivion's veil;
Let's consider the past with a lingering gaze,
Like a peacock whose eyes are inclined to his tail.

Aye, come, let us turn our attention behind,
Like those critics whose heads are so heavy, I fear,
That they cannot keep up with the march of the mind,
And so turn face about for reviewing the rear.

Looking over Time's crupper and over his tail,
Oh, what ages and pages there are to revise!
And as further our back-searching glances prevail,
Like the emmets, "how little we are in our eyes!"

What a sweet pretty innocent, half-a-yard long,
On a dimity lap of true nursery make!
I can fancy I hear the old lullaby song
That was meant to compose me, but kept me awake.

Methinks I still suffer the infantine throes,
When my flesh was a cushion for any long pin—
Whilst they patted my body to comfort my woes,
Oh! how little they dreamt they were driving them in!

Infant sorrows are strong—infant pleasures as weak—
But no grief was allowed to indulge in its note;
Did you ever attempt a small "bubble and squeak,"
Thro' the Dalby's Carminative down in your throat?

Did you ever go up to the roof with a bounce?
Did you ever come down to the floor with the same?
Oh! I can't but agree with both ends, and pronounce
"Head or tails," with a child, an unpleasantish game?

Then an urchin — I see myself urchin, indeed,
With a smooth Sunday face for a mother's de-
light:
Why should weeks have an end? — I am sure
there was need
Of a Sabbath, to follow each Saturday night.

Was your face ever sent to the housemaid to scrub?
Have you ever felt huckaback softened with
sand?
Had you ever your nose towelled up to a snub,
And your eyes knuckled out with the back of
the hand?

Then a school-boy — my tailor was nothing in
fault,
For an urchin will grow to a lad by degrees,—
But how well I remember that "pepper and salt"
That was down to the elbows, and up to the
knees!

What a figure it cut when as Norval I spoke!
With a lanky right leg duly planted before;
Whilst I told of the chief that was killed by my
stroke,
And extended *my* arms as "the arms that he
wore!"

Next a Lover — Oh! say were you ever in love?
With a lady too cold — and your bosom too hot?

Have you bowed to a shoe-tie, and knelt to a glove?
  Like a *beau* that desired to be tied in a knot?

With the Bride all in white, and your body in blue,
  Did you walk up the aisle — the genteelest of men?
When I think of that beautiful vision anew,
  Oh! I seem but the *biffin* of what I was then!

I am withered and worn by a premature care,
  And my wrinkles confess the decline of my days;
Old Time's busy hand has made free with my hair,
  And I'm seeking to hide it — by writing for bays!

A BUTCHER.

WHOE'ER has gone thro' London Street,
Has seen a butcher gazing at his meat,
    And how he keeps
    Gloating upon a sheep's
Or bullock's personals, as if his own;
    How he admires his halves
    And quarters — and his calves,
As if in truth upon his own legs grown; —

His fat! *his* suet!
His kidneys peeping elegantly thro' it!
His thick flank!
And *his* thin!
His shank!
His shin!
Skin of his skin, and bone too of his bone!

With what an air
He stands aloof, across the thoroughfare,
Gazing — and will not let a body by,
Tho' buy! buy! buy! be constantly his cry
Meanwhile with arms akimbo, and a pair
Of Rhodian legs, he revels in a stare
At his Joint Stock — for one may call it so,
Howbeit, without a *Co.*
The dotage of self-love was never fonder
Than he of his brute bodies all a-row;
Narcissus in the wave did never ponder,
With love so strong,
On his "portrait charmant,"
As our vain Butcher on his carcass yonder.

Look at his sleek round skull!
How bright his cheek, how rubicund his nose is
His visage seems to be
Ripe for beef-tea;
Of brutal juices the whole man is full —
In fact, fulfilling the metempsychosis,
The butcher is already half a Bull.

"DON'T YOU SMELL FIRE."

RUN ! — run for St. Clements's engine !
 For the Pawnbroker's all in a blaze,
And the pledges are frying and singing —
 Oh ! how the poor pawners will craze !
Now where can the turncock be drinking ?
 Was there ever so thirsty an elf ? —
But he still may tope on, for I'm thinking
 That the plugs are as dry as himself.

The engines ! — I hear them come rumbling ;
 There's the Phœnix ! the Globe ! and the Sun !
What a row there will be, and a grumbling,
 When the water don't start for a run !
See ! there they come racing and tearing,
 All the street with loud voices is filled ;
Oh ! it's only the firemen a-swearing
 At a man they've run over and killed !

How sweetly the sparks fly away now,
 And twinkle like stars in the sky ;
It's a wonder the engines don't play now,
 But I never saw water so shy !

Why there isn't enough for a snipe,
  And the fire it is fiercer, alas!
Oh! instead of the New River pipe,
  They have gone — that they have — to the gas.

Only look at the poor little P——'s
  On the roof — is there any thing sadder?
My dears, keep fast hold, if you please,
  And they won't be an hour with the ladder!
But if any one's hot in their feet,
  And in very great haste to be saved,
Here's a nice easy bit in the street,
  That M'Adam has lately unpaved!

There is some one — I see a dark shape
  At that window, the hottest of all,—
My good woman, why dont you escape?
  Never think of your bonnet and shawl:
If your dress isn't perfect, what is it
  For once in a way to your hurt?
When your husband is paying a visit
  There, at Number Fourteen, in his shirt!

Only see how she throws out her *chaney!*
  Her basons, and teapots, and all
The most brittle of *her* goods — or any,
  But they all break in breaking their fall:
Such things are not surely the best
  From a two-story window to throw —
She might save a good iron-bound chest,
  For there's plenty of people below!

O dear! what a beautiful flash!
  How it shone thro' the window and door;
We shall soon hear a scream and a crash,
  When the woman falls thro' with the floor!
There! there! what a volley of flame,
  And then suddenly all is obscured! —
Well — I'm glad in my heart that I came; —
  But I hope the poor man is insured!

THE WIDOW.

One widow at a grave will sob
A little while, and weep, and sigh!
If two should meet on such a job,
They'll have a gossip by and by.
If three should come together — why,
Three widows are good company!
If four should meet by any chance,
Four is a number very nice,
To have a rubber in a trice —
But five will up and have a dance!

Poor Mrs. C——— (why should I not
Declare her name? — her name was Cross)
Was one of those the "common lot"
Had left to weep "no common loss:" —
For she had lately buried then
A man the "very best of men,"

A lingering truth, discovered first
Whenever men "are at the worst."
To take the measure of her woe,
It was some dozen inches deep —
I mean in crape, and hung so low,
It hid the drops she did *not* weep:
In fact, what human life appears,
It was a perfect "veil of tears."
Though ever since she lost "her prop
And stay," — alas! he wouldn't stay —
She never had a tear to mop,
Except one little angry drop,
From Passion's eye, as Moore would say;
Because, when Mister Cross took flight,
It looked so very like a spite —
He died upon a washing-day!
Still Widow Cross went twice a week,
As if "to wet a widow's cheek,"
And soothe his grave with sorrow's gravy,—
'Twas nothing but a make-believe,
She might as well have hoped to grieve
Enough of brine to float a navy;
And yet she often seemed to raise
A cambric kerchief to her eye —
A *duster* ought to be the phrase,
Its work was all so very dry.
The springs were locked that ought to flow —
In England or in widow-woman —
As those that watch the weather know,
Such "backward Springs" are not uncommon.

But why did Widow Cross take pains,
To call upon the "dear remains,"—
Remains that could not tell a jot,
Whether she ever wept or not,
Or how his relict took her losses?
Oh! my black ink turns red for shame—
But still the naughty world must learn,
There was a little German came
To shed a tear in "Anna's Urn,"
At the next grave to Mr. Cross's!
For there an angel's virtues slept,
"Too soon did Heaven assert its claim!"
But still her painted face he kept,
"Encompassed in an angel's frame."

He looked quite sad and quite deprived,
His head was nothing but a hat-band;
He looked so lone, and so *un*wived,
That soon the Widow Cross contrived
To fall in love with even *that* band;
And all at once the brackish juices
Came gushing out thro' sorrow's sluices—
Tear after tear too fast to wipe,
Tho' sopped, and sopped, and sopped again—
No leak in sorrow's private pipe,
But like a bursting on the main!
Whoe'er has watched the window-pane—
I mean to say in showery weather—
Has seen two little drops of rain,
Like lovers very fond and fain,

At one another creeping, creeping,
Till both, at last, embrace together:
So fared it with that couple's weeping,
The principle was quite as active —
    Tear unto tear
    Kept drawing near,
Their very blacks became attractive.
To cut a shortish story shorter,
Conceive them sitting tête-à-tête —
Two cups,— hot muffins on a plate,—
With "Anna's Urn" to hold hot water!
The brazen vessel for a while,
Had lectured in an easy song,
Like Abernethy — on the bile —
The scalded herb was getting strong;
All seemed as smooth as smooth could be,
To have a cosy cup of tea;
Alas! how often human sippers
With unexpected bitters meet,
And buds, the sweetest of the sweet,
Like sugar, only meet the nippers!

The Widow Cross, I should have told,
Had seen three husbands to the mould;
She never sought an Indian pyre,
Like Hindoo wives that lose their loves,
But with a proper sense of fire,
Put up, instead, with "three removes:"
Thus, when with any tender words

Or tears she spoke about her loss,
The dear departed, Mr. Cross,
Came in for nothing but his thirds;
For, as all widows love too well,
She liked upon the list to dwell,
And oft ripped up the old disasters —
She might, indeed, have been supposed
A great *ship* owner, for she prosed
Eternally of her Three Masters!
Thus, foolish woman! while she nursed
Her mild souchong, she talked and reckoned
What had been left her by her first,
And by her last, and by her second.
Alas! not all her annual rents
Could then entice the little German —
Not Mr. Cross's three Per Cents,
Or Consols, ever make him *her* man;
He liked her cash, he liked her houses,
But not that dismal bit of land
She always settled on her spouses.
So taking up his hat and band,
Said he, "You'll think my conduct odd —
But here my hopes no more may linger;
I thought you had a wedding-finger,
But oh! — it is a curtain-rod!"

ODE TO THE CAMELEOPARD.

WELCOME to Fredom's birthplace — and a den!
Great Anti-climax, hail!
So very lofty in thy front — but then,
So dwindling at the tail! —
In truth, thou hast the most unequal legs!
Has one pair galloped, whilst the other trotted,
Along with other brethren, leopard-spotted,
O'er Afric sand, where ostriches lay eggs?
Sure thou wert caught in some hard up-hill chase,
Those hinder heels still keeping thee in check!
And yet thou seemest prepared in any case,
Tho' they had lost the race,
To win it by a neck!
That lengthy neck — how like a crane's it looks!
Art thou the overseer of all the brutes?
Or dost thou browse on tip-top leaves or fruits —
Or go a-birdnesting amongst the rooks?
How kindly nature caters for all wants;
Thus giving unto thee a neck that stretches,
And high food fetches —
To some a long nose, like the elephant's!

Oh! hadst thou any organ to thy bellows,
To turn thy breath to speech in human style,
What secrets thou mightst tell us,
Where now our scientific guesses fail;
For instance, of the Nile,
Whether those Seven Mouths have any tail —
Mayhap thy luck too,
From that high head, as from a lofty hill,
Has let thee see the marvellous Timbuctoo —
Or drink of Niger at its infant rill;
What were the travels of our Major Denham,
Or Clapperton, to thine
In that same line,
If thou couldst only squat thee down and pen 'em!

Strange sights, indeed, thou must have overlooked,
With eyes held ever in such vantage-stations!
Hast seen, perchance, unhappy white folks cooked,
And then made free of negro corporations!
Poor wretches saved from cast-away three-deckers,
By sooty wreckers —
From hungry waves to have a loss still drearier,
To far exceed the utmost aim of Park!
And find themselves, alas! beyond the mark,
In the *insides* of Africa's Interior!

Live on, Giraffe! genteelest of raff kind!
Admired by noble, and by royal tongues!
May no pernicious wind,
Or English fog, blight thy exotic lungs!

Live on in happy peace, altho' a rarity,
Nor envy thy poor cousin's more outrageous
Parisian popularity ; —
Whose very leopard-rash is grown contagious,
And worn on gloves and ribbons all about,
Alas ! they 'll wear him out ! —
So thou shalt take thy sweet diurnal feeds —
When he is stuffed with undigested straw,
Sad food that never visited his jaw !
And staring round him with a brace of beads !

ODE TO DR. HAHNEMANN, THE HOMŒOPATHIST.

Well, Doctor,
Great concoctor
Of medicines to help in man's distress ;
Diluting down the strong to meek,
And making even the weak more weak,
" Fine by degrees, and beautifully less " —
Founder of a new system economic,
To druggists any thing but comic ;
Framed the whole race of Ollapods to fret,
At profits, like thy doses, very small ;
To put all Doctors' Boys in evil case,
Thrown out of bread, of physic, and of place, —
And show us old Apothecaries' Hall
" To Let. "

How fare thy Patients? are they dead or living,
Or, well as can expected be, with such
A style of practice, liberally giving
"A sum of more to that which had too much?"
Dost thou preserve the human frame, or turf it?
Do thorough draughts cure thorough colds or not?
Do fevers yield to any thing that 's hot?
Or hearty dinners neutralize a surfeit?
Is 't good advice for gastronomic ills,
When Indigestion's face with pain is crumpling,
To cry, "Discard those Peristaltic Pills,
Take a hard dumpling?"

Tell me, thou German Cousin,
And tell me honestly without a diddle,
Does an attenuated dose of rosin
Act as a *tonic* on the old *Scotch fiddle?*
Tell me, when Anhalt-Coethen babies wriggle,
Like eels just caught by sniggle,
Martyrs to some acidity internal,
That gives them pangs infernal,
Meanwhile the lip grows black, the eye enlarges;
Say, comes there all at once a cherub-calm,
Thanks to that soothing homœopathic balm,
The half of half, of half, a drop of "*varges?*"

Suppose, for instance, upon Leipzig's plain,
A soldier pillowed on a heap of slain,
In urgent want both of a priest and proctor;
When lo! there comes a man in green and red,

A featherless cocked-hat adorns his head,
In short, a Saxon military doctor —
Would he, indeed, on the right treatment fix,
 To cure a horrid gaping wound,
 Made by a ball that weighed a pound,
If he well peppered it with number six?

Suppose a felon doomed to swing
 Within a *rope*,
 Might friends not hope
To cure him with a *string?*
Suppose his breath arrived at a full stop,
The shades of death in a black cloud before him,
Would a quintillionth dose of the New Drop
 Restore him?
Fancy a man gone rabid from a bite,
 Snapping to left and right,
And giving tongue like one of Sebright's hounds,
 Terrific sounds,
The pallid neighborhood with horror cowing,
To hit the proper homœopathic mark;
Now, might not "the last taste in life" of *bark*,
 Stop his *bow-wow-ing?*
Nay, with a well-known remedy to fit him,
Would he not mend, if, with all proper care,
 He took "*a hair*
Of the dog that bit him?"

Picture a man — we 'll say a Dutch Meinheer —
 In evident emotion,
Bent o'er the bulwark of the Batavier.

Owning those symptoms queer —
Some feel in a *Sick Transit* o'er the ocean,
Can any thing in life be more pathetic
Than when he turns to us his wretched face? —
But would it mend his case
To be decillionth-dosed
With something like the ghost
Of an emetic?

Lo! now a darkened room!
Look through the dreary gloom,
And see that coverlet of wildest form,
Tost like the billows in a storm,
Where ever and anon, with groans, emerges
A ghastly head! —
While two impatient arms still beat the bed,
Like a strong swimmer's struggling with the surges;
There Life and Death are on their battle-plain,
With many a mortal ecstasy of pain —
What shall support the body in its trial,
Cool the hot blood, wild dream, and parching skin,
And tame the raging Malady within —
A sniff of Next-to-Nothing in a phial?

Oh! Doctor Hahnemann, if here I laugh,
And cry together, half and half,
Excuse me, 'tis a mood the subject brings,
To think, whilst I have crowed like chanticleer,
Perchance, from some dull eye the hopeless tear

Hath gushed with my light levity at schism,
To mourn some Martyr of Empiricism.
Perchance, on thy system, I have given
A pang, superfluous to the pains of Sorrow,
Who weeps with Memory from morn till even;
Where comfort there is none to lend or borrow,
Sighing to one sad strain,
"She will not come again,
To-morrow, nor to-morrow, nor to-morrow!"

Doctor forgive me, if I dare prescribe
A rule for thee thyself, and all thy tribe,
Inserting a few serious words by stealth;
Above all price of wealth
The Body's Jewel,—not for minds profane,
Or hands, to tamper with in practice vain—
Like to a Woman's Virtue is Man's Health.
A heavenly gift within a holy shrine!
To be approached and touched with serious fear,
By hands made pure, and hearts of faith severe,
Even as the Priesthood of the ONE divine!

But, zounds! each fellow with a suit of black,
And, strange to fame,
With a diplomaed name,
That carries two more letters pick-a-back,
With cane, and snuffbox, powdered wig, and block,
Invents *his* dose, as if it were a chrism,
And dares to treat our wondrous mechanism,

Familiar as the works of old Dutch clock;
Yet, how would common sense esteem the man,
Oh how, my unrelated German cousin,
Who having some such time-keeper on trial,
And finding it too fast, enforced the dial,
To strike upon the Homœopathic plan
Of fourteen to the dozen.

Take my advice, 'tis given without a fee,
Drown, drown your book ten thousand fathoms deep,
Like Prospero's beneath the briny sea,
For spells of magic have all gone to sleep!
Leave no decillionth fragment of your works,
To help the interest of quacking Burkes;
Aid not in murdering even widow's mites,—
And now forgive me for my candid zeal,
I had not said so much, but that I feel
Should you *take ill* what here my Muse indites,
An Ode-ling more will set you all to rights.

A CUSTOM-HOUSE BREEZE.

One day — no matter for the month or year,
A Calais packet, just come over,
And safely moored within the pier,
Began to land her passengers at Dover;

All glad to end a voyage long and rough,
And during which,
Through roll and pitch,
The Ocean-King had *sick*ophants enough!

Away, as fast as they could walk or run,
Eager for steady rooms and quiet meals,
With bundles, bags, and boxes at their heels
Away the passengers all went, but one,
A female, who from some mysterious check,
Still lingered on the steamer's deck,
As if she did not care for land a tittle,
For horizontal rooms, and cleanly victual —
Or nervously afraid to put
Her foot
Into an Isle described as "tight and little."

In vain commissioner and touter,
Porter and waiter thronged about her;
Boring, as such officials only bore —
In spite of rope and barrow, knot, and truck,
Of plank and ladder, there she stuck,
She couldn't, no she wouldn't go on shore.

"But, ma'am," the steward interfered,
"The wessel must be cleared.
You musn't stay aboard, ma'am, no one don't!
It's quite agin the orders so to do —
And all the passengers is gone but you."
Says she, "I cannot go ashore and won't!"

"You ought to!"
  "But I can't!"
"You must!"
  "I shan't!"

At last, attracted by the racket
  'Twixt gown and jacket,
 The captain came himself, and cap in hand,
 Begged very civilly to understand
Wherefore the lady could not leave the packet.

"Why then," the lady whispered with a shiver,
 That made the accents quiver,
  "I've got some foreign silks about me pinned,
 In short so many things, all contraband,
 To tell the truth I am afraid to land,
  In such a *searching* wind!"

UP THE RHINE.

Ye Tourists and Travellers, bound to the Rhine,
Provided with passport, that requisite docket,
First listen to one little whisper of mine —
Take care of your pocket! — take care of your pocket!

Don't wash or be shaved — go like hairy wild men,
Play dominoes, smoke, wear a cap, and smock-
frock it,
But if you speak English, or look it, why then
Take care of your pocket! — take care of your
pocket!

You 'll sleep at great inns, in the smallest of beds,
Find charges as apt to mount up as a rocket,
With thirty per cent. as a tax on your heads,
Take care of your pocket! — take care of your
pocket!

You 'll see old Cologne,— not the sweetest of
towns,—
Wherever you follow your nose you will shock it;
And you 'll pay your three dollars to look at three
crowns,
Take care of your pocket! — take care of your
pocket!

You 'll count seven Mountains, and see Roland's
Eck,
Hear legends veracious as any by Crockett;
But oh! to the tone of romance what a check,
Take care of your pocket! — take care of your
pocket!

Old Castles you 'll see on the vine-covered hill,—
Fine ruins to rivet the eye in its socket —

Once haunts of Baronial Banditti,—and still
Take care of your pocket! — take care of your
pocket!

You'll stop at Coblence, with its beautiful views,
But make no long stay with your money to stock
it,
Where Jews are all Germans, and Germans all
Jews,
Take care of your pocket! — take care of your
pocket!

A Fortress you'll see, which, as people report,
Can never be captured, save famine should block
it —
Ascend Ehrenbreitstein — but that's not their
forte,
Take care of your pocket! — take care of your
pocket!

You'll see an old man who'll let off an old gun,
And Lurley, with her hurly-burly, will mock it;
But think that the words of the echo thus run,
Take care of your pocket! — take care of your
pocket!

You'll gaze on the Rheingau, the soil of the
Vine!
Of course you will freely Moselle it and Hock
it —

P'raps purchase some pieces of Humbugheim wine —
Take care of your pocket! — take care of your pocket!

Perchance you will take a frisk off to the Baths —
Where some to their heads hold a pistol and cock it;
But still mind the warning, wherever your paths,
Take care of your pocket! — take care of your pocket!

And Friendships you 'll swear most eternal of pacts,
Change rings, and give hair to be put in a locket;
But still, in the most sentimental of acts,
Take care of your pocket! — take care of your pocket!

In short, if you visit that stream or its shore,
Still keep at your elbow one caution to knock it,
And where Schinderhannes was Robber of yore,
Take care of your pocket! — take care of your pocket!

TO * * * * *

WITH A FLASK OF RHINE WATER.

THE old Catholic City was still,
In the Minster the vespers were sung,
And, re-echoed in cadences shrill,
The last call of the trumpet had rung ;
While, across the broad stream of the Rhine,
The full Moon cast a silvery zone ;
And, methought, as I gazed on its shine,
" Surely, this is the Eau de Cologne."

I inquired not the place of its source,
If it ran to the east or the west ;
But my heart took a note of its course,
That it flowed towards Her I love best —
That it flowed towards Her I love best,
Like those wandering thoughts of my own ;
And the fancy such sweetness possessed,
That the Rhine seemed all Eau de Cologne !

THE KNIGHT AND THE DRAGON.

In the famous old times,
(Famed for chivalrous crimes,)
As the legends of Rhineland deliver,
Once there flourished a Knight,
Who Sir Otto was hight,
On the banks of the rapid green river!

On the Drachenfels' crest
He had built a stone nest,
From which he pounced down like a vulture,
And with talons of steel
Out of every man's meal
Took a very extortionate multure.

Yet he lived in good fame,
With a nobleman's name,
As "Your-High-and-Well-Born" addressed daily —
Tho' Judge Park in his wig,
Would have deemed him a prig,
Or a cracksman, if tried at the Old Bailey.

It is strange — very strange!
How opinions will change! —

How Antiquity blazons and hallows
Both the man and the crime
That a less lapse of time
Would commend to the hulks or the gallows!

Thus enthralled by Romance,
In a mystified trance,
E'en a young, mild, and merciful Woman
Will recall with delight
The wild Keep, and its Knight,
Who was quite as much Tiger as Human!

Now it chanced on a day,
In the sweet month of May,
From his casement Sir Otto was gazing,
With his sword in the sheath,
At that prospect beneath,
Which our Tourists declare so amazing!

Yes — he gazed on the Rhine,
And its banks, so divine;
Yet with no admiration or wonder,
But the goût of a thief,
As a more modern Chief
Looked on London, and cried "What a plunder!"

From that river so fast,
From that champaign so vast,
He collected rare tribute and presents;

Water-rates from ships' loads,
Highway-rates on the roads,
And hard Poor-rates from all the poor Peas-
ants!

When behold! round the base
Of his strong dwelling-place,
Only gained by most toilsome progression,
He perceived a full score
Of the rustics or more,
Winding up in a sort of procession!

"Keep them out!" the Knight cried,
To the Warders outside —
But the Hound at his feet gave a grumble!
And in scrambled the knaves,
Like Feudality's slaves,
With all forms that are servile and humble.

"Now for boorish complaints!
Grant me patience, ye Saints!"
Cried the Knight, turning red as a mullet;
When the baldest old man
Thus his story began,
With a guttural croak in his gullet!

"Lord Supreme of our lives,
Of our daughters, our wives,
Our she-cousins, our sons, and their spouses,
Of our sisters and aunts,

Of the babies God grants,
Of the handmaids that dwell in our houses!

"Mighty master of all
We possess, great or small,
Of our cattle, our sows, and their farrows;
Of our mares and their colts,
Of our crofts, and our holts,
Of our ploughs, of our wains, and our harrows!

"Noble Lord of the soil,
Of its corn and its oil,
Of its wine, only fit for such gentles!
Of our carp and sour-kraut,
Of our carp and our trout,
Our black bread, and black puddings, and lentils!

"Sovran Lord of our cheese,
And whatever you please —
Of our bacon, our eggs, and our butter,
Of our backs and our polls,
Of our bodies and souls —
O give ear to the woes that we utter!

"We are truly perplexed,
We are frighted and vexed,
Till the strings of our heart are all twisted;
We are ruined and curst,

By the fiercest and worst
Of all Robbers that ever existed!"

"Now by Heaven and this light!"
In a rage cried the Knight,
"For this speech all your bodies shall stiffen
What! by Peasants miscalled!"
Quoth the man that was bald,
"Not your honor we mean, but a Griffin.

"For our herds and our flocks,
He lays wait in the rocks;
And jumps forth without giving us warning;
Two poor wethers, right fat,
And four lambs after that,
Did he swallow this very May morning!"

Then the High-and-Well-Born
Gave a laugh as in scorn,
"Is the Griffin indeed such a glutton?
Let him eat up the rams,
And the lambs, and their dams —
If I hate any meat it is mutton!"

"Nay, your Worship," said then
The most bald of old men,
"For a sheep we would hardly thus cavil;
If the merciless Beast
Did not oftentimes feast
On the Pilgrims, and people that travel."

"Feast on what?" cried the Knight,
Whilst his eye glistened bright
With the most diabolical flashes —
"Does the Beast dare to prey
On the road and highway?
With our proper diversion that clashes!"

"Yea, 'tis so, and far worse,"
Said the Clown, "to our curse;
For by way of a snack or a tiffin,
Every week in the year,
Sure as Sundays appear,
A young Virgin is thrown to the Griffin!"

"Ha! Saint Peter! Saint Mark!"
Roared the Knight, frowning dark,
With an oath that was awful and bitter:
"A young maid to his dish!
Why what more could he wish,
If the Beast were High Born, and a Ritter!

"Now by this our good brand,
And by this our right hand,
By the badge that is borne on our banners,
If we can but once meet
With the Monster's retreat,
We will teach him to poach on our Manors!"

Quite content with this vow,
With a scrape and a bow,

The glad Peasants went home to their flagons,
Where they tippled so deep,
That each clown in his sleep
Dreamt of killing a legion of Dragons!

Thus engaged, the bold Knight
Soon prepared for the fight
With the wily and scaly marauder;
But ere battle began,
Like a good Christian man,
First he put all his household in order.

"Double bolted and barred
Let each gate have a guard"—
(Thus his rugged Lieutenant was bidden;)
"And be sure, without fault,
No one enters the vault
Where the Church's gold vessels are hidden.

"In the dark Oubliette,
Let yon Merchant forget
That he e'er had a bark richly laden —
And that desperate youth,
Our own rival forsooth!
Just indulge with a Kiss of the Maiden!

"Crush the thumbs of the Jew
With the vice and the screw,
Till he tells where he buried his treasure;
And deliver our word

To yon sullen caged Bird,
That to-night she must sing for our pleasure !"

Thereupon, cap-a-pee,
As a Champion should be,
With the bald-headed Peasant to guide him,
On his War-horse he bounds,
And then, whistling his hounds,
Prances off to what fate may betide him !

Nor too long do they seek,
Ere a horrible reek,
Like the fumes from some villanous tavern,
Sets the dogs on the snuff,
For they scent well enough,
The foul Monster coiled up in his cavern!

Then alighting with speed
From his terrified steed,
Which he ties to a tree for the present,
With his sword ready drawn,
Strides the Ritter High-born,
And along with him drags the scared peasant!

" O Sir Knight, good Sir Knight!
I am near enough quite —
I have shown you the Beast and his grotto; "
But before he can reach
Any further in speech,
He is stricken stone-dead by Sir Otto!

Who withdrawing himself
To a high rocky shelf,
Sees the Monster his tail disentangle
From each tortuous coil,
With a sudden turmoil,
And rush forth the dead Peasant to mangle.

With his terrible claws,
And his horrible jaws,
He soon moulds the warm corse to a jelly;
Which he quickly sucks in
To his own wicked skin
And then sinks at full stretch on his belly.

Then the Knight softly goes,
On the tips of his toes,
To the greedy and slumbering Savage,
And with one hearty stroke
Of his sword, and a poke,
Kills the Beast that had made such a ravage.

So, extended at length,
Without motion or strength,
That gorged Serpent they call the Constrictor,
After dinner, while deep
In lethargical sleep,
Falls a prey to his Hottentot victor.

"'Twas too easy by half!"
Said the Knight, with a laugh;

"But as nobody witnessed the slaughter,
I will swear, knock and knock,
By Saint Winifred's clock,
We were at it three hours and a quarter!"

Then he chopt off the head
Of the Monster so dread,
Which he tied to his horse as a trophy;
And, with Hounds, by the same
Ragged path that he came,
Home he jogged proud as Sultan or Sophy!

Blessed Saints! what a rout
When the news flew about,
And the carcase was fetched in a wagon;
What an outcry rose wild
From man, woman, and child —
"Live Sir Otto, who vanquished the Dragon!"

All that night the thick walls
Of the Knights feudal halls
Rang with shouts for the wine-cup and flagon;
Whilst the Vassals stood by,
And repeated the cry —
"Live Sir Otto, who vanquished the Dragon!"

The next night, and the next,
Still the fight was the text,
'Twas a theme for the Minstrels to brag on!
And the Vassals' hoarse throats

Still re-echoed the notes —
" Live Sir Otto who vanquished the Dragon ! "

There was never such work
Since the days of King Stork,
When he lived with the Frogs at free quarters !
Not to name the invites
That were sent down of nights,
To the villagers' wives and their daughters !

It was feast upon feast,
For good cheer never ceased,
And a foray replenished the flagon ;
And the Vassals stood by,
But more weak was the cry —
" Live Sir Otto, who vanquished the Dragon ! "

Down again sank the sun,
Nor were revels yet done —
But as if every mouth had a gag on,
Tho' the Vassals stood round,
Deuce a word or a sound
Of " Sir Otto who vanquished the Dragon ! "

There was feasting aloft,
But, thro' pillage so oft,
Down below there was wailing and hunger ;
And affection ran cold,
And the food of the old,
It was wolfishly snatched by the younger !

Mad with troubles so vast,
Where 's the wonder at last
If the Peasants quite altered their motto ? —
And with one loud accord
Cried out "Would to the Lord
That the Dragon had vanquished Sir Otto ! "

OUR LADY'S CHAPEL.

A LEGEND OF COBLENZ.

WHOE'ER has crossed the Mósel Bridge,
And mounted by the fort of Kaiser Franz,
Has seen, perchance,
Just on the summit of St. Peter's ridge,
A little open chapel to the right,
Wherein the tapers aye are burning bright;
So popular, indeed, this holy shrine,
At least among the female population,
By night, or at high noon, you see it shine,
A very Missal for *illumination !*

Yet, when you please, at morn or eve, go by
All other Chapels, standing in the fields,
Whose mouldy, wifeless husbandry but yields
Beans, peas, potatoes, mangel-wurzel, rye,

And lo! the Virgin, lonely, dark, and hush,
Without the glimmer of a farthing rush!

But on Saint Peter's Hill
The lights are burning, burning, burning still.
In fact, it is a pretty retail trade
To furnish forth the candles ready made;
And close beside the chapel and the way,
A chandler, at her stall, sits day by day,
And sells, both long and short, the waxen tapers,
Smartened with tinsel-foil and tinted papers.

To give of the mysterious truth an inkling,
Those who in this bright chapel breathe a prayer
To "Unser Frow," and burn a taper there,
Are said to get a husband in a twinkling:
Just as she-glow-worms, if it be not scandal,
Catch partners with *their* matrimonial candle.

How kind of blessed saints in heaven —
Where none in marriage, we are told, are given —
To interfere below in making matches,
And help old maidens to connubial catches!
The truth is, that instead of looking smugly
(At least, so whisper wags satirical)
The votaries are all so old and ugly,
No man could fall in love but by a miracle,

However, that such waxen gifts and vows
Are sometimes for the purpose efficacious,
In helping to a spouse,.
Is vouched for by a story most veracious.

A certain Woman, though in name a wife,
Yet doomed to lonely life,
Her truant husband having been away
Nine years, two months, a week, and half a day,—
Without remembrances by words or deeds,—
Began to think she had sufficient handle
To talk of widowhood and burn her weeds,
Of course with a wax-candle.
Sick, single-handed with a world to grapple,
Weary of solitude, and spleen, and vapors,
Away she hurried to Our Lady's Chapel,
Full-handed with *two* tapers —
And prayed as she had never prayed before,
To be a bona fide wife once more.
"Oh Holy Virgin! listen to my prayer!
And for sweet mercy, and thy sex's sake,
Accept the vows and offerings I make —
Others set up one light, but here 's *a pair!*"

Her prayer, it seemed, was heard;
For in three little weeks, exactly reckoned,
As blithe as any bird,
She stood before the Priest with Hans the Second; —

A fact that made her gratitude so hearty,
To "Unser Frow," and her propitious shrine,
She sent two waxen candles superfine,
Long enough for a Lapland evening party!

Rich was the Wedding Feast and rare —
What sausages were there!
Of sweets and sours there was a perfect glut:
With plenteous liquors to wash down good cheer
Brantwein, and Rhum, Kirsch-wasser, and Krug Bier,
And wine so *sharp* that every one was *cut.*
Rare was the feast — but rarer was the quality
Of mirth, of smoky-joke, and song, and toast,—
When just in all the middle of their jollity —
With bumpers filled to Hostess and to Host,
And all the unborn branches of their house,
Unwelcome and unasked, like Banquo's Ghost,
In walked the long-lost Spouse!

What pen could ever paint
The hubbub when the Hubs were thus confronted!
The bridesmaids fitfully began to faint;
The bridesmen stared — some whistled and some grunted:
Fierce Hans the First looked like a boar that's hunted;
Poor Hans the Second like a suckling calf:

Meanwhile, confounded by the double miracle,
The twofold bride sobbed out, with tears hysterical,
"Oh Holy Virgin, you 're too good — *by half!*"

MORAL.

Ye Cóblenz maids, take warning by the rhyme,
And as our Christian laws forbid polygamy,
For fear of bigamy,
Only light up *one* taper at a time.

LOVE LANGUAGE OF A MERRY YOUNG SOLDIER.

(FROM THE GERMAN.)

" *Ach, Gretchen, mein täubchen.*"

O Gretel, my Dove, my heart's Trumpet,
My Cannon, my Big Drum, and also my Musket,
O hear me, my mild little Dove,
In your still little room.

Your portrait, my Gretel, is always on guard,
Is always attentive to Love's parole and watchword;

Your picture is always going the rounds,
My Gretel, I call at every hour!

My heart's Knapsack is always full of you;
My looks, they are quartered with you;
And when I bite off the top end of a cartridge,
Then I think that I give you a kiss.

You alone are my Word of Command and orders,
Yea, my Right-face, Left-face, Brown Tommy, and wine,
And at the word of command "Shoulder Arms!"
Then I think you say, "Take me in your arms."

Your eyes sparkle like a Battery,
Yea, they wound like Bombs and Grenades;
As black as Gunpowder is your hair,
Your hand as white as Parading breeches!

Yes, you are the Match and I am the Cannon;
Have pity, my love, and give quarter,
And give the word of command, "Wheel round
Into my heart's Barrack Yard."

TOWN AND COUNTRY.

AN ODE.

IMITATED FROM HORACE.

Oh! well may poets make a fuss
In summer time, and sigh "*O rus!*"
  Of London pleasures sick:
My heart is all at pant to rest
In greenwood shades — my eyes detest
  This endless meal of brick!

What joy have I in June's return?
My feet are parched, my eyeballs burn,
  I scent no flowery gust:
But faint the flagging zephyr springs,
With dry Macadam on its wings,
  And turns me "dust to dust."

My sun his daily course renews
Due east, but with no Eastern dews;
  The path is dry and hot!
His setting shows more tamely still,
He sinks behind no purple hill,
  But down a chimney's pot!

Oh! but to hear the milkmaid blithe;
Or early mower whet his scythe
The dewy meads among! —
My grass is of that sort — alas,
That makes no hay — called sparrow-grass
By folks of vulgar tongue!

Oh! but to smell the woodbines sweet!
I think of cowslip cups — but meet
With very vile rebuffs!
For meadow-buds I get a whiff
Of Cheshire cheese,— or only sniff
The turtle made at Cuff's.

How tenderly Rousseau reviewed
His periwinkles! — mine are strewed!
My rose blooms on a gown! —
I hunt in vain for eglantine,
And find my blue-bell on the sign
That marks the Bell and Crown:

Where are ye, birds! that blithely wing
From tree to tree, and gayly sing
Or mourn in thickets deep?
My cuckoo has some ware to sell,
The watchman is my Philomel,
My blackbird is a sweep!

Where are ye, linnet, lark, and thrush!
That perch on leafy bough and bush,

And tune the various song?
Two hurdy-gurdists, and a poor
Street-Handel grinding at my door
Are all my "tuneful throng."
Where are ye, early-purling streams,
Whose waves reflect the morning beams
And colours of the skies?
My rills are only puddle-drains
From shambles, or reflect the stains
Of calimanco-dyes!

Sweet are the little brooks that run
O'er pebbles glancing in the sun,
Singing in soothing tones: —
Not thus the city streamlets flow;
They make no music as they go,
Though never "off the stones."

Where are ye, pastoral pretty sheep,
That wont to bleat, and frisk, and leap
Beside your woolly dams?
Alas! instead of harmless crooks,
My Corydons use iron hooks,
And skin — not shear — the lambs.

The pipe whereon, in olden day,
The Arcadian herdsman used to play
Sweetly — here soundeth not;
But merely breathes unwholesome fumes,
Meanwhile the city boor consumes
The rank weed — "piping hot."

All rural things are vilely mocked,
On every hand the sense is shocked
   With objects hard to bear:
Shades — vernal shades! — where wine is sold!
And for a turfy bank, behold
   An Ingram's rustic chair!

Where are ye, London meads and bowers,
And gardens redolent of flowers
   Wherein the zephyr wons!
Alas! Moor Fields are fields no more:
See Hatton's Garden bricked all o'er;
   And that bare wood — St. John's.

No pastoral scenes procure me peace;
I hold no Leasowes in my lease,
   No cot set round with trees:
No sheep-white hill my dwelling flanks;
And omnium furnishes my banks
   Who brokers — not with bees.

Oh! well may poets make a fuss
In summer time, and sigh "*O rus!*"
   Of city pleasures sick:
My heart is all at pant to rest
In greenwood shades — my eyes detest
   That endless meal of brick!

LAMENT FOR THE DECLINE OF CHIVALRY.

WELL hast thou cried, departed Burke,
All chivalrous romantic work
Is ended now and past! —
That iron age — which some have thought
Of mettle rather overwrought —
Is now all overcast!

Ay — where are those heroic knights
Of old — those armadillo wights
Who wore the plated vest,—
Great Charlemagne and all his peers
Are cold — enjoying with their spears
An everlasting rest!

The bold king Arthur sleepeth sound,
So sleep his knights who gave that Round
Old Table such eclat!
Oh, Time has plucked the plumy brow!
And none engage at Turney's now
But those that go to law!

Grim John o'Gaunt is quite gone by,
And Guy is nothing but a Guy,
Orlando lies forlorn! —
Bold Sidney, and his kidney — nay,
Those "early champions" — what are they
But knights without a morn.

No Percy branch now perseveres
Like those of old in breaking spears —
The name is now a lie! —
Surgeons, alone, by any chance,
Are all that ever couch a lance
To couch a body's eye!

Alas for Lion-Hearted Dick!
That cut the Moslems to the quick,
His weapon lies in peace:
Oh, it would warm them in a trice,
If they could only have a spice
Of his old mace in Greece!

The famed Rinaldo lies a-cold,
And Tancred too, and Godfrey bold,
That scaled the holy wall!
No Saracen meets Paladin,
We hear of no great *Saladin*,
But only grow the small!

Our *Cressys* too have dwindled since
To penny things — at our Black Prince

Historic pens would scoff:
The only one we moderns had,
Was nothing but a Sandwich lad,
And measles took him off!

Where are those old and feudal clans,
Their pikes, and bills, and partisans:
Their hauberks — jerkins — buffs?
A battle was a battle then,
A breathing piece of work; but men
Fight now — with powder puffs!

The curtal-axe is out of date!
The good old cross-bow bends — to Fate,
'Tis gone — the archer's craft!
No tough arm bends the springing yew,
And jolly draymen ride, in lieu
Of Death, upon the shaft!

The spear — the gallant tilter's pride,
The rusty spear, is laid aside,
Oh, spits now domineer!
The coat of mail is left alone,—
And where is all chain armour gone?
Go ask at Brighton Pier.

We fight in ropes, and not in lists,
Bestowing handcuffs with our fists,
A low and vulgar art!
No mounted man is overthrown:

A tilt! it is a thing unknown —
Except upon a cart!

Methinks I see the bounding barb,
Clad like his chief in steely garb,
For warding steel's appliance!
Methinks I hear the trumpet stir!
'Tis but the guard to Exeter,
That bugles the "Defiance!"

In cavils when will cavaliers
Set ringing helmets by the ears,
And scatter plumes about?
Or blood — if they are in the vein?
That tap will never run again —
Alas, the *Casque* is out!

No iron-crackling now is scored
By dint of battle-axe or sword,
To find a vital place —
Though certain doctors still pretend,
Awhile, before they kill a friend,
To labor through his case!

Farewell then ancient men of might!
Crusader, errant-squire, and knight!
Our coats and custom soften,—
To rise would only make you weep —
Sleep on, in rusty-iron sleep,
As in a safety coffin!

THE GREEN MAN.

TOM SIMPSON was as nice a kind of man
As ever lived — at least at number Four,
In Austin Friars in Mrs. Brown's first floor,
At fifty pounds,— or thereabouts,— per ann.
The lady reckoned him her best of lodgers,
His rent so punctually paid each quarter,—
He did not smoke like nasty foreign codgers,—
 Or play French horns like Mr. Rogers —
Or talk his flirting nonsense to her daughter,—
Not that the girl was light behaved or courtable —
Still, on one failing tenderly to touch,
The Gentleman did like a drop too much,
 (Though there are many such,)
And took more Port than was exactly portable.
In fact,— to put the cap upon the nipple,
And try the charge,— Tom certainly *did* tipple.

Once in the company of merry mates,
In spite of Temperance's ifs and buts,
So sure as Eating is set off with *plates*,
His drinking always was bound up with *cuts!*
 Howbeit, such Bacchanalian revels
Bring very sad catastrophes about.

Poor Simpson! what a thing occurred to him!
'Twas Christmas — he had drunk the night
before,—
Like Baxter, who so "went beyond his last" —
One bottle more, and then *one* bottle more,
Till oh! the red-wine *Ruby-con* was passed!
And homeward, by the short small chimes of day,
With many a circumbendibus to spare,
For instance, twice round Finsbury Square,
To use a fitting phrase, he *wound* his way.

Then comes the rising, with repentance bitter,
And all the nerves — (and sparrows) — in a twitter,
Till settled by the sober Chinese cup:
The hands, o'er all are members that make motions,
A sort of wavering, just like the ocean's,
Which has its swell, too, when its getting up —
An awkward circumstance enough for elves
Who shave themselves,
And Simpson just was ready to go through it,
When lo! the first short glimpse within the glass —
He jumped — and who alive would fail to do it?
To see, however it had come to pass,
One section of his face as green as grass!
In vain each eager wipe,
With soap — without — wet — hot or cold — or dry,
Still, still, and still, to his astonished eye,
One cheek was green, the other cherry ripe!
Plump in the nearest chair he sat him down,
Quaking, and quite absorbed in a deep study,—

But verdant and not brown,—
What could have happened to a tint so ruddy?
Indeed it was a very novel case,
By way of penalty for being jolly,
To have that evergreen stuck in his face,
Just like the windows with their Christmas holly.

"All claret marks,"—thought he—Tom knew his forte—
"Are red—this colour CANNOT come from Port!"

One thing was plain; with such a face as his,
'Twas quite impossible to ever greet
Good Mrs. Brown.

—So he tied up his head,
As with raging tooth, and took to bed:
Of course with feelings far from the serene,
For all his future prospects seemed to be,
To match his customary tea,
Black, mixt with green.

Meanwhile, good Mrs. Brown
Wondered at Mr. S. not coming down,
And sent the maid up stairs to learn the why;
To whom poor Simpson, half delirious,
Returned an answer so mysterious
That curiosity began to fry;
The more, as Betty, who had caught a snatch
By peeping in upon the patient's bed,

Reported a most bloody, tied-up head,
Got over-night of course—"Harm watch, harm catch,"
From Watchmen in a boxing match.

So, liberty or not,—
Good lodgers are too scarce to let them off in
A suicidal coffin—
The dame ran up as fast as she could trot;
Appearance,—"fiddle-sticks!" should not deter
From going to the bed,
And looking at the head;
La! Mister S——, he need not care for her!
A married woman that had had
Nine boys and gals, and none had turned out bad—
Her own dear late would come home late at nigh
And liquor always got him in a fight.
She'd been in hospitals—she wouldn't faint
At gores and gashes fingers wide and deep;
She knew what's good for bruises and what ain't—
Turlington's Drops she made a pint to keep.
Cases she'd seen beneath the surgent's hand—
Such skulls japanned—she meant to say trepanned!

Hereat she plucked the white cravat aside,
And lo! the whole phenomenon was seen—
"Preserve us all! He's going to gangrene!"
Alas! through Simpson's brain
Shot the remark, like ball, with mortal pain;

It tallied truly with his own misgiving,
And brought a groan,
To move a heart of stone —
A sort of farewell to the land of living!
And as the case was imminent and urgent,
He did not make a shadow of objection
To Mrs. B.'s proposal for a "surgent."

Swift flew the summons,— it was life or death!
And in as short a time as he could race it,
Came Doctor Puddicome, as short of breath,
To try his Latin charms against *Hic Jacet*,
He took a seat beside the patient's bed,
Saw tongue — felt pulse — examined cheek,—
Poked, stroked, pinched, kneaded it — hemmed — shook his head —
Took a long solemn pause the cause to seek,
(Thinking, it seemed, in Greek,)
Then asked — 'twas Christmas — "Had he eaten grass,
Or greens — and if the cook was so improper
To boil them up with copper,
Or farthings made of brass,
Or if he drank his Hock from dark green glass,
Or dined at City Festivals, whereat
There 's turtle, and green fat?"
To all of which, with serious tone of woe,
Poor Simpson answered "No."
The Doctor was at fault;
A thing so new quite brought him to a halt.
Cases of other colours came in crowds.

Black with Black Jaundice he had seen the skin;
From Yellow Jaundice yellow,
From saffron tints to sallow.
Even those eruptions he had never seen
Of which the Caledonian Poet spoke,
As "*rashes* growing green"—
"Phoo! phoo! a rash grow green!
Nothing of course but a broad Scottish joke!"
Then as to flaming visages, for those
The Scarlet fever answered, or the Rose—
But verdant! that was quite a novel stroke!

So matters stood in-doors—meanwhile without
Growing in going like all other rumours,
The modern miracle was buzzed about.

"Green faces!" so they all began to comment—
"Yes—opposite to Druggists' lighted shops,
But that's a flying colour—never stops—
A bottle-green, that's vanished in a moment.
Green! nothing of the sort occurs to mind—
Nothing at all to match the present piece;
Jack in the Green has nothing of the kind—
Green-grocers are not green, nor yet green geese!"
The oldest Supercargoes or Old Sailors
Of such a case had never heard,
From Emerald Isle to Cape de Verd;
"Or Greenland!" cried the whalers.

All tongues were full of the Green Man, and still
They could not make him out, with all their skill.
No soul could shape the matter, head or tail —
But Truth steps in where all conjectures fail.

A long half hour, in needless puzzle,
Our Galen's cane had rubbed against his muzzle ;
He thought, and thought, and thought, and thought,
and thought —
And still it came to nought,
When up rushed Betty, loudest of Town Criers,
" Lord, Ma'am, the new Police is at the door !
It's B, Ma'am, Twenty-four,—
As brought home Mister S. to Austin Friars,
And says there's nothing but a simple case,
He got that 'ere green face
By sleeping in the kennel near the Dyer's ! "

MORE HULLAHBALOO.

Loud as from numbers without number.

MILTON.

You may do it extempore, for it 's nothing but roaring.

QUINCE.

AMONGST the great inventions of this age,
  Which every other century surpasses,
Is one,—just now the rage,—
  Called "Singing for all classes"—
That is, for all the British millions,
      And billions,
      And quadrillions,
      Not to name *Quintilians,*
That now, alas! have no more ear than asses,
  To learn to warble like the birds in June.
      In time and tune,
Correct as clocks, and musical as glasses!

  In fact, a sort of plan,
Including gentleman as well as yokel,
  Public or private man,
To call out a Militia,—only Vocal
      Instead of Local,

And not designed for military follies,
  But keeping still within the civil border,
  To form with mouths in open order,
    And sing in volleys.

Whether this grand harmonic scheme
Will ever get beyond a dream,
  And tend to British happiness and glory,
    Maybe no, and maybe yes,
    Is more than I pretend to guess —
  However, here 's my story.

In one of those small, quiet streets,
    Where Business retreats,
To shun the daily bustle and the noise
    The shoppy Strand enjoys,
But Law, Joint Companies, and Life Assurance
    Find past endurance —
In one of those back streets, to Peace so dear,
  The other day, a ragged wight
  Began to sing with all his might,
"*I have a silent sorrow here!*"

The place was lonely; not a creature stirred
Except some little dingy bird;
Or vagrant cur that snuffed along
Indifferent to the Son of Song;
No truant errand-boy, or Doctor's lad,
No idle Filch or lounging cad,
  No pots encumbered with diurnal beer,

No printer's devil with an author's proof,
Or housemaid on an errand far aloof,
  Lingered the tattered Melodist to hear —
Who yet, confound him! bawled as loud
As if he had to charm a London crowd,
  Singing beside the public way,
Accompanied — instead of violin,
Flute, or piano, chiming in —
  By rumbling cab, and omnibus, and dray,
A van with iron bars to play *staccato*,
    Or engine *obligato* —
In short, without one instrument vehicular
(Not even a truck, to be particular,)
  There stood the rogue and roared,
  Unasked and unencored,
Enough to split the organs called auricular!

Heard in that quiet place,
Devoted to a still and studious race,
  The noise was quite appalling!
To seek a fitting simile and spin it,
  Appropriate to his calling,
His voice had all Lablache's *body* in it;
But oh! the scientific tone it lacked,
    And was, in fact,
Only a forty-boatswain-power of bawling!

'Twas said, indeed, for want of vocal *nous*,
  The stage had banished him when he tempted
    it,

For tho' his voice completely filled the house,
It also emptied it.
However, there he stood
Vociferous — a ragged don!
And with his iron pipes laid on
A row to all the neighbourhood.

In vain were sashes closed
And doors against the persevering Stentor,
Though brick, and glass, and solid oak opposed,
Th' intruding voice would enter,
Heedless of ceremonial or decorum,
Den, office, parlour, study, and sanctorum;
Where clients and attorneys, rogues, and fools,
Ladies, and masters who attended schools,
Clerks, agents, all provided with their tools,
Were sitting upon sofas, chairs, and stools,
With shelves, pianos, tables, desks, before 'em —
How it did bore 'em!

Louder, and louder still,
The fellow sang with horrible good-will,
Curses both loud and deep his sole gratuities,
From scribes bewildered making many a flaw
In deeds of law
They had to draw;
With dreadful incongruities
In posting ledgers, making up accounts
To large amounts,
Or casting up annuities —

Stunned by that voice, so loud and hoarse,
Against whose overwhelming force
No invoice stood a chance, of course!

The Actuary pshawed and "pished,"
And knit his calculating brows, and wished
The singer "a bad life"—a mental murther!
The Clerk, resentful of a blot and blunder,
    Wished the musician further,
    Poles distant—and no wonder!
For Law and Harmony tend far asunder—
The lady could not keep her temper calm,
Because the sinner did not sing a psalm—
The Fiddler in the very same position
    As Hogarth's chafed musician
(Such prints require but cursory reminders)
Came and made faces at the wretch beneath,
And wishing for his foe between his teeth,
    (Like all impatient elves
    That spite themselves)
  Ground his own Grinders.

But still with unrelenting note,
  Though not a copper came of it, in verity,
The horrid fellow with the ragged coat,
      And iron throat,
Heedless of present honour and posterity,
Sang like a Poet singing for prosperity,
      In penniless reliance—
And, sure, the most immortal Man of Rhyme

Never set Time
More thoroughly at defiance!

From room to room, from floor to floor,
From Number One to Twenty-four
The nuisance bellowed, till all patience lost,
Down came Miss Frost,
Expostulating at her open door —
"Peace, monster, peace!
Where *is* the New Police!
I vow I cannot work, or read, or pray,
Don't stand there bawling, fellow, don't!
You really send my serious thoughts astray,
Do — there's a dear good man — do, go away."
Says he, "I won't!"

The spinster pulled her door to with a slam,
That sounded like a wooden d—n,
For so some moral people, strictly loth
To swear in words, however up,
Will crash a curse in setting down a cup,
Or through a doorpost vent a banging oath —
In fact, this sort of physical transgression
Is really no more difficult to trace
Than in a given face
A very bad expression.

However, in she went,
Leaving the subject of her discontent
To Mr. Jones's Clerk at Number Ten;

Who, throwing up the sash,
With accents rash,
Thus hailed the most vociferous of men:
"Come, come, I say old fellor, stop your chant:
I cannot write a sentence — no one can't!
So just pack up your trumps,
And stir your stumps —"
Says he, "I shant!"

Down went the sash
As if devoted to "eternal smash,"
(Another illustration
Of acted imprecation,)
While close at hand, uncomfortably near,
The independent voice, so loud and strong,
And clanging like a gong,
Roared out again the everlasting song,
"I have a silent sorrow here!"

The thing was hard to stand!
The Music-master could not stand it —
But rushing forth with fiddlestick in hand,
As savage as a bandit,
Made up directly to the tattered man,
And thus in broken sentences began,
But playing first a prelude of grimaces,
Twisting his features to the strangest shapes,
So that to guess his subject from his faces,
He meant to give a lecture upon apes —

"Com — com — I say!
You go away!
Into two parts my head you split —
My fiddle cannot hear himself a bit,
When I do play —
You have no bis'ness in a place so still!
Can you not come another day?"
Says he — "I will."

"No — no — you scream and bawl!
You must not come at all!
You have no rights, by rights, to beg —
You have not one off leg —
You ought to work — you have not some com- [plaint —
You are not cripple in your back or bones —
Your voice is strong enough to break some stones" —
Says he — "It aint!"

"I say you ought to labour!
You are in a young case,
You have not sixty years upon your face,
To come and beg your neighbour,
And discompose his music with a noise
More worse than twenty boys —
Look what a street it is for quiet!
No cart to make a riot,
No coach, no horses, no postilion,
If you will sing, I say, it is not just
To sing so loud." — Says he, "I MUST!
I'm SINGING FOR THE MILLION!"

ODES AND ADDRESSES.

ODE TO MR. GRAHAM.

THE AERONAUT.

"Up with me!—up with me into the sky!"
WORDSWORTH—*on a Lark!*

DEAR Graham, whilst the busy crowd,
The vain, the wealthy, and the proud,
Their meaner flights pursue,
Let us cast off the foolish ties
That bind us to the earth, and rise
And take a bird's-eye view!—

A few more whiffs of my segar
And then, in Fancy's airy car,
Have with thee for the skies:—
How oft this fragrant smoke upcurled
Hath borne me from this little world,
And all that in it lies!—

Away!—away!—the bubble fills—
Farewell to earth and all its hills!—

We seem to cut the wind!—
So high we mount, so swift we go,
The chimney tops are far below,
The Eagle's left behind!—

Ah me! my brain begins to swim!—
The world is growing rather dim;
The steeples and the trees—
My wife is getting very small!
I cannot see my babe at all!—
The Dollond, if you please!

Do, Graham, let me have a quiz,
Lord! what a Lilliput it is,
That little world of Mogg's!—
Are those the London Docks?—that channel,
The mighty Thames?—a proper kennel
For that small Isle of Dogs!—

What is that seeming tea-urn there?
That fairy dome, St. Paul's!—I swear,
Wren must have been a Wren!—
And that small stripe?—it cannot be
The City Road!—Good lack! to see
The little ways of men!

Little, indeed!—my eyeballs ache
To find a turnpike.—I must take
Their tolls upon my trust!—
And where is mortal labor gone?

Look, Graham, for a little stone
  Mac Adamized to dust!

Look at the horses!—less than flies!—
Oh, what a waste it was of sighs
  To wish to be a Mayor!
What is the honor?—none at all,
One's honor must be very small
  For such a civic chair!—

And there's Guildhall!—'tis far aloof—
Methinks, I fancy through the roof
  Its little guardian Gogs,
Like penny dolls—a tiny show!—
Well—I must say they're ruled below
  By very little logs!—

Oh! Graham, how the upper air
Alters the standards of compare;
  One of our silken flags
Would cover London all about—
Nay, then—let's even empty out
  Another brace of bags!

Now for a glass of bright Champagne
Above the clouds!—Come, let us drain
  A bumper as we go!—
But hold!—for God's sake do not cant
The cork away—unless you want
  To brain your friends below.

Think! what a mob of little men
Are crawling just within our ken,
 Like mites upon a cheese!—
Pshaw!—how the foolish sight rebukes
Ambitious thoughts!—can there be *Dukes*
 Of *Gloster* such as these!—

Oh! what is glory?—what is fame?
Hark to the little mob's acclaim,
 'T is nothing but a hum!—
A few near gnats would trump as loud
As all the shouting of a crowd
 That has so far to come!—

Well—they are wise that choose the near,
A few small buzzards in the ear,
 To organs ages hence!—
Ah me! how distance touches all;
It makes the true look rather small,
 But murders poor pretence.

"The world recedes—it disappears!
Heaven opens on my eyes—my ears
 With buzzing noises ring!"—
A fig for Southey's Laureat lore!—
What 's Rogers here?—Who cares for Moore
 That hears the Angels sing!—

A fig for earth, and all its minions!—
We are above the world's opinions,

Graham! we 'll have our own!—
Look what a vantage height we've got—
Now——*do* you think Sir Walter Scott
Is such a Great Unknown?

Speak up!—or hath he hid his name
To crawl thro' "subways" unto fame,
Like Williams of Cornhill?—
Speak up, my lad!—when men run small
We 'll show what 's little in them all,
Receive it how they will!—

Think now of Irving!—shall he preach
The princes down—shall he impeach
The potent and the rich,
Merely on ethic stilts—and I
Not moralize at two miles high—
The true didactic pitch!

Come:—what d' ye think of Jeffrey, sir?
Is Gifford such a Gulliver
In Lilliput's Review,
That like Colossus he should stride
Certain small brazen inches wide
For poets to pass through?

Look down! the world is but a spot.
Now say—Is Blackwood's *low* or not,
For all the Scottish tone?
It shall not weigh us here—not where

The sandy burden's lost in air—
  Our lading—where is 't flown?

Now—like you Croly's verse indeed—
In heaven—where one cannot read
  The "Warren" on a wall?
What think you here of that man's fame?
Tho' Jerdan magnified his name,
  To me 'tis very small!

And, truly, is there such a spell
In those three letters, L. E. L.,
  To witch a world with song?
On clouds the Byron did not sit,
Yet dared on Shakspeare's head to spit,
  And say the world was wrong!

And shall not we? Let's think aloud!
Thus being couched upon a cloud,
  Graham, we'll have our eyes!
We felt the great when we were less,
But we'll retort on littleness
  Now we are in the skies.

O Graham, Graham! how I blame
The bastard blush—the petty shame
  That used to fret me quite—
The little sores I covered then,
No sores on earth, nor sorrows when
  The world is out of sight!

My name is Tims.—I am the man
That North's unseen, diminished clan
  So scurvily abused!
I am the very P. A. Z.
The London Lion's small pin's head
  So often hath refused!

Campbell—(you cannot see him here)—
Hath scorned my *lays* :—do his appear
  Such great eggs from the sky?—
And Longman, and his lengthy Co.
Long, only, in a little Row,
  Have thrust my poems by!

What else?—I 'm poor, and much beset
With damned small duns—that is—in debt
  Some grains of golden dust!
But only worth, above, is worth.—
What 's all the credit of the earth!
  An inch of cloth on trust!

What 's Rothschild here, that wealthy man!
Nay, worlds of wealth?—Oh, if you can
  Spy out— the *Golden Ball!*
Sure as we rose, all money sank:
What 's gold or silver now?—the Bank
  Is gone—the 'Change and all!

What 's all the ground-rent of the globe?—
Oh, Graham, it would worry Job

To hear its landlords prate!
But after this survey, I think
I 'll ne'er be bullied more, nor shrink
From men of large estate!

And less, still less, will I submit
To poor mean acres' worth of wit—
I that have heaven's span—
I that like Shakspeare's self may dream
Beyond the very clouds, and seem
An Universal Man!

Mark, Graham, mark those gorgeous crowds!
Like Birds of Paradise the clouds
Are winging on the wind!
But what is grander than their range?
More lovely than their sun-set change?—
The free creative mind!

Well! the Adults' School 's in the air!
The greatest men are lessoned there
As well as the Lessee!
Oh could Earth's Ellistons thus small
Behold the greatest stage of all,
How humbled they would be!

"Oh would some Power the giftie gie 'em,
To see themselves as others see 'em,"
'T would much abate their fuss!
If they could think that from the skies

They are as little in our eyes
   As they can think of us!

Of us? are we gone out of sight?
Lessened! diminished! vanished quite!
   Lost to the tiny town!
Beyond the Eagle's ken—the grope
Of Dollond's longest telescope!
   Graham! we're going down!

Ah me! I've touched a string that opes
The airy valve!—the gas elopes—
   Down goes our bright Balloon!—
Farewell the skies! the clouds! I smell
The lower world! Graham, farewell,
   Man of the silken moon!.

The earth is close! the City nears—
Like a burnt paper it appears,
   Studded with tiny sparks!
Methinks I hear the distant rout
Of coaches rumbling all about—
   We're close above the Parks!

I hear the watchmen on their beats,
Hawking the hour about the streets.
   Lord! what a cruel jar
It is upon the earth to light!
Well—there's the finish of our flight!
   I've smoked my last segar!

ODE TO MR. M'ADAM.

"Let us take to the road!"—BEGGAR'S OPERA.

M'ADAM, hail!
Hail, Roadian! hail, Colossus! who dost stand
Striding ten thousand turnpikes on the land!
Oh universal Leveller! all hail!
To thee, a good, yet stony-hearted man,
The kindest one, and yet the flintiest going—
To thee—how much for thy commodious plan,
Lanark Reformer of the Ruts, is Owing!
The Bristol mail
Gliding o'er ways, hitherto deemed invincible,
When carrying Patriots now shall never fail
Those of the most "*unshaken* public principle."
Hail to thee, Scot of Scots!
Thou northern light, amid those heavy men!
Foe to Stonehenge, yet friend to all beside,
Thou scatterest flints and favors far and wide,
From palaces to cots;—
Dispenser of coagulated good!
Distributor of granite and of food!
Long may thy fame its even path march on

E'en when thy sons are dead!
Best benefactor! though thou giv'st a stone
To those who ask for bread!

Thy first great trial in this mighty town
Was, if I rightly recollect, upon
That gentle hill which goeth
Down from "the County" to the Palace gate,
And, like a river, thanks to thee, now floweth
Past the Old Horticultural Society—
The chemist Cobb's, the house of Howell and James,
Where ladies play high shawl and satin games—
A little *Hell* of lace!
And past the Athenæum, made of late,
Severs a sweet variety
Of milliners and booksellers who grace
Waterloo Place,
Making division, the Muse fears and guesses,
'Twixt Mr. Rivington's and Mr. Hessey's.
Thou stood'st thy trial, Mac! and shaved the road
From Barber Beaumont's to the King's abode
So well, that paviors threw their rammers by,
Let down their tucked shirt-sleeves, and with a sigh
Prepared themselves, poor souls, to chip or die!

Next, from the palace to the prison, thou
Didst go, the highway's watchman, to thy beat—

Preventing though the *rattling* in the street,
Yet kicking up a row
Upon the stones—ah! truly watchman-like,
Encouraging thy victims all to strike,
To further thy own purpose, Adam, daily;—
Thou hast smoothed, alas, the path to the Old Bailey!
And to the stony bowers
Of Newgate, to encourage the approach,
By caravan or coach—
Hast strewed the way with flints as soft as flowers.
Who shall dispute thy name!
Insculpt in stone in every street,
We soon shall greet
Thy trodden down, yet all unconquered fame!
Where'er we take, even at this time, our way,
Nought see we, but mankind in open air,
Hammering thy fame, as Chantrey would not dare;—
And with a patient care
Chipping thy immortality all day!
Demosthenes, of old—that rare old man—
Prophetically *followed*, Mac! thy plan:—
For he, we know,
(History says so,)
Put *pebbles* in his mouth when he would speak
The *smoothest* Greek!

It is "impossible, and cannot be,"
But that thy genius hath,

Besides the turnpike, many another path
Trod, to arrive at popularity,
O'er Pegasus, perchance, thou hast thrown a thigh,
Nor ridden a roadster only; mighty Mac!
And 'faith I 'd swear, when on that winged hack,
Thou hast observed the highways in the sky!
Is the path up Parnassus rough and steep,
And "hard to climb," as Dr. B. would say?
Dost think it best for Sons of Song to keep
The noiseless *tenor* of their way? (see Gray.)
What line of road *should* poets take to bring
Themselves unto those waters, loved the first!—
Those waters which can wet a man to sing!
Which, like thy fame, "from *granite* basins burst,
Leap into life, and, sparkling, woo the thirst?"
That thou 'rt a proser, even thy birthplace might
Vouchsafe;—and Mr. Cadell *may*, God wot,
Have paid thee many a pound for many a blot—
Cadell 's a wayward wight!
Although no Walter, still thou art a Scot,
And I can throw, I think, a little light
Upon some works thou hast written for the town—
And published, like a Lilliput Unknown!
"Highways and Byeways," is thy book, no doubt,

(One whole edition 's out,)
And next, for it is fair
That Fame,
Seeing her children, should confess she had
'em:—
"Some *Passages* from the life of Adam Blair"—
(Blair is a Scottish name,)
What are they, but thy own good roads, M'Adam?

O! indefatigable laborer
In the paths of men! when thou shalt die, 't will
be
A mark of thy surpassing industry,
That of the monument, which men shall rear
Over thy most inestimable bone,
Thou didst thy very self lay the first stone!—
Of a right ancient line thou comest—through
Each crook and turn we trace the unbroken clue,
Until we see thy sire before our eyes—
Rolling his gravel walks in Paradise!
But he, our great Mac Parent, erred, and ne'er
Have our walks since been fair!
Yet Time, who, like the merchant, lives on
'Change,
Forever varying, through his varying range,
Time maketh all things even!
In this strange world, turning beneath high
heaven!
He hath redeemed the Adams, and contrived—
(How are Time's wonders hived!)

In pity to mankind and to befriend 'em—
(Time is above all praise)
That he, who first did make our evil ways,
Reborn in Scotland, should be first to mend 'em!

A FRIENDLY ADDRESS

TO MRS. FRY, IN NEWGATE.

"Sermons in stones."—As you Like It.
"Out! out! damned spot!"—Macbeth.

I like you, Mrs. Fry! I like your name!
It speaks the very warmth you feel in pressing
In daily act round Charity's great flame—
I like the crisp Browne way you have of dress-
ing,
Good Mrs. Fry! I like the placid claim
You make to Christianity—professing
Love, and good *works*—of course you buy of Bar-
ton,
Beside the young *fry's* booksellers, Friend Dar-
ton!

I like good Mrs. Fry, your brethren mute—
Those serious, solemn gentlemen that sport—

I should have said, that *wear*, the sober suit
Shaped like a court dress—but for heaven's court.
I like your sisters too—sweet Rachel's fruit—
Protestant nuns! I like their stiff support
Of virtue—and I like to see them clad
With such a difference—just like good from bad!

I like the sober colors—not the wet;
Those gaudy manufactures of the rainbow—
Green, orange, crimson, purple, violet—
In which the fair, the flirting, and the vain, go—
The others are a chaste, severer set,
In which the good, the pious, and the plain, go—
They 're moral *standards*, to know Christians by—
In short, they are your *colors*, Mrs. Fry!

As for the naughty tinges of the prism—
Crimson's the cruel uniform of war—
Blue—hue of brimstone! minds no catechism;
And green is young and gay—not noted for
Goodness, or gravity, or quietism,
Till it is saddened down to tea-green, or
Olive—and purple 's given to wine, I guess;
And yellow is a convict by its dress!

They 're all the devil's liveries, that men
And women wear in servitude to sin—

But how will they come off, poor motleys, when
  Sin's wages are paid down, and they stand in
The Evil Presence! You and I know, then
  How all the party colors will begin
To part—the *Pit*tite hues will sadden there,
Whereas the *Fox*ite shades will all show fair!

Witness their goodly labors one by one!
  Russet makes garments for the needy poor—
Dove-color preaches love to all—and *dun*
  Calls every day at Charity's street-door—
Brown studies Scripture, and bids women shun
  All gaudy furnishing—*olive* doth pour
Oil into wounds: and *drab* and *slate* supply
Scholar and book in Newgate, Mrs. Fry!

Well! Heaven forbid that I should discommend
  The gratis, charitable, jail-endeavor!
When all persuasions in your praises blend—
  The Methodist's creed and cry are, *Fry* for-
      ever!
No—I will be your friend—and, like a friend,
  Point out your very worst defect—Nay, never
Start at that word! But I *must* ask you why
You keep your school *in* Newgate, Mrs. Fry?

Too well I know the price our mother Eve
  Paid for *her* schooling: but must all her daugh-
      ters
Commit a petty larceny, and thieve—

Pay down a crime for "*entrance*" to your
"*quarters?*"
Your classes may increase, but I must grieve
Over your pupils at their bread and waters!
Oh, tho' it cost you rent—(and rooms run high)
Keep your school *out* of Newgate, Mrs. Fry!

O save the vulgar soul before it 's spoiled!
Set up your mounted sign *without* the gate—
And there inform the mind before 'tis soiled!
'Tis sorry writing on a greasy slate!
Nay, if you would not have your labors foiled,
Take it *inclining* towards a virtuous state,
Not prostrate and laid flat—else, woman meek!
The *upright* pencil will but hop and shriek!

Ah, who can tell how hard it is to drain
The evil spirit from the heart it preys in—
To bring sobriety to life again,
Choked with the vile Anacreontic raisin—
To wash Black Betty when her black's ingrain—
To stick a moral lacquer on Moll Brazen,
Of Suky Tawdry's habits to deprive her;
To tame the wild-fowl ways of Jenny Diver!

Ah, who can tell how hard it is to teach
Miss Nancy Dawson on her bed of straw—
To make long Sal sew up the endless breach
She made in manners—to write heaven's own
law

On hearts of granite.—Nay, how hard to preach,
In cells, that are not memory's—to draw
The moral thread, thro' the immoral eye
Of blunt Whitechapel natures, Mrs. Fry!

In vain you teach them baby-work within:
'Tis but a clumsy botchery of crime;
'Tis but a tedious darning of old sin—
Come out yourself, and stitch up souls in time—
It is too late for scouring to begin
When virtue 's ravelled out, when all the prime
Is worn away, and nothing sound remains;
You 'll fret the fabric out before the stains!

I like your chocolate, good Mistress Fry!
I like your cookery in every way;
I like your shrove-tide service and supply;
I like to hear your sweet *Pandeans* play;
I like the pity in your full-brimmed eye;
I like your carriage, and your silken gray,
Your dove-like habits, and your silent preaching;
But I don't like your Newgatory teaching.

Come out of Newgate, Mrs. Fry! Repair
Abroad, and find your pupils in the streets.
O, come abroad into the wholesome air,
And take your moral place, before Sin seats
Her wicked self in the Professor's chair.
Suppose some morals raw! the true receipt's

To dress them in the pan, but do not try
To cook them in the fire, good Mrs. Fry!

Put on your decent bonnet, and come out!
  Good lack! the ancients did not set up schools
In jail—but at the *Porch!* hinting, no doubt,
  That Vice should have a lesson in the rules
Before 't was whipt by law.—O come about,
  Good Mrs. Fry! and set up forms and stools
All down the Old Bailey, and thro' Newgate-
    street,
But not in Mr. Wontner's proper seat!

Teach Lady Barrymore, if, teaching, you
  That peerless Peeress can absolve from dolor;
Teach her it is not virtue to pursue
  Ruin of blue, or any other color;
Teach her it is not Virtue's crown to rue,
  Month after month, the unpaid drunken dollar;
Teach her that "flooring Charleys" is a game
Unworthy one that bears a Christian name.

O come and teach our children—that ar'n't *ours*—
  That heaven's straight pathway is a narrow way,
Not Broad St. Giles's, where fierce Sin devours
  Children, like Time—or rather they both prey
On youth together—meanwhile Newgate low'rs
  Even like a black cloud at the close of day,
To shut them out from any more blue sky:
Think of these hopeless wretches, Mrs. Fry!

You are not nice—go into their retreats,
And make them Quakers, if you will.—'T were best
They wore straight collars, and their shirts sans *pleats;*
That they had hats *with* brims—that they were drest
In garbs without *lappels*—than shame the streets
With so much raggedness.—You may invest
Much cash this way—but it will cost its price,
To give a good, round, real *cheque* to Vice!

In brief—Oh teach the child its moral rote,
Not *in* the way from which 't will not depart—
But *out*—out—out! Oh, bid it walk remote!
And if the skies are closed against the smart,
Even let him wear the single-breasted coat,
For that ensureth singleness of heart.—
Do what you will, his every want supply,
Keep him—but *out* of Newgate, Mrs. Fry!

ODE TO RICHARD MARTIN, ESQUIRE,

M.P. FOR GALWAY.

"*Martin*, in this, has proved himself a very good Man!"—
BOXIANA.

How many sing of wars,
Of Greek and Trojan jars—
The butcheries of men!
The Muse hath a "Perpetual Ruby Pen!"
Dabbling with heroes and the blood they spill;
But no one sings the man
That, like a pelican,
Nourishes Pity with his tender *Bill!*

Thou Wilberforce of hacks!
Of whites as well as blacks,
Piebald and dapple gray,
Chestnut and bay—
No poet's eulogy thy name adorns!
But oxen, from the fens,
Sheep—in their pens,
Praise thee, and red cows with their winding horns!

Thou art sung on brutal pipes!
Drovers may curse thee,
Knackers asperse thee,
And sly M.P.'s bestow their cruel wipes;
But the old horse neighs thee,
And zebras praise thee,
Asses, I mean—that have as many stripes!

Hast thou not taught the Drover to forbear,
In Smithfield's muddy, murderous, vile environ—
Staying his lifted bludgeon in the air!
Bullocks don't wear
Oxide of iron!
The cruel Jarvy thou hast summoned oft,
Enforcing mercy on the coarse Yahoo,
That thought his horse the *courser* of the two—
Whilst Swift smiled down aloft!—
O worthy pair! for this, when ye inhabit
Bodies of birds—(if so the spirit shifts
From flesh to feather)—when the clown uplifts
His hands against the sparrows nest, to *grab* it—
He shall not harm the MARTINS and the *Swifts!*

Ah! when Dean Swift was *quick*, how he enhanced
The horse!—and humbled biped man like Plato!
But now he 's dead, the charger is mischanced—
Gone backward in the world—and not advanced—
Remember Cato!

Swift was the horse's champion—not the King's
Whom Southey sings,
Mounted on Pegasus—would he were thrown!
He 'll wear that ancient hackney to the bone,
Like a mere clothes-horse airing royal things!
Ah well-a-day! the ancients did not use
Their steeds so cruelly!—let it debar men
From wonted rowelling and whip's abuse—
Look at the ancients' *Muse!*
Look at their *Carmen!*

O, Martin! how thine eye—
That one would think had put aside its lashes—
That can't bear gashes
Thro' any horse's side, must ache to spy
That horrid window fronting Fetter-lane—
For there 's a nag the crows have picked for victual,
Or some man painted in a bloody vein—
Gods! is there no *Horse-spital!*
That such raw shows must sicken the humane!
Sure Mr. Whittle
Loves thee but little,
To let that poor horse linger in his *pane!*

O build a Brookes's Theatre for horses!
O wipe away the national reproach—
And find a decent Vulture for their corses!
And in thy funeral track
Four sorry steeds shall follow in each coach!

Steeds that confess "the luxury of *woe!*"
True mourning steeds, in no extempore black,
And many a wretched hack
Shall sorrow for thee—sore with kick and blow
And bloody gash—it is the Indian knack—
(Save that the savage is his own tormentor)—
Banting shall weep too in his sable scarf—
The biped woe the quadruped shall enter,
And Man and Horse go half and half,
As if their griefs met in a common *Centaur!*

ODE TO THE GREAT UNKNOWN.

"O breathe not his name!"—MOORE.

THOU Great Unknown!
I do not mean Eternity, nor Death,
That vast incog!
For I suppose thou hast a living breath,
Howbeit we know not from whose lungs 'tis blown,
Thou man of fog!
Parent of many children—child of none!
Nobody's son!
Nobody's daughter—but a parent still!
Still but an ostrich parent of a batch
Of orphan eggs—left to the world to hatch.
Superlative Nil!

A vox and nothing more—yet not Vauxhall;
A head in papers, yet without a curl!
Not the Invisible Girl!
No hand—but a handwriting on a wall—
A popular nonentity,
Still called the same—without identity!
A lark, heard out of sight—
A nothing shined upon—invisibly bright,
"Dark with excess of light!"
Constable's literary John-a-nokes—
The real Scottish wizard—and not witch,
Nobody—in a niche;
Every one's hoax!
Maybe Sir Walter Scott—
Perhaps not!
Why dost thou so conceal and puzzle curious folks?

Thou—whom the second-sighted never saw,
The Master Fiction of fictitious history!
Chief Nong tong paw!
No mister in the world—and yet all mystery!
The "tricksy spirit" of a Scotch Cock Lane—
A *novel* Junius puzzling the world's brain—
A man of Magic—yet no talisman!
A man of clair obscure—not he o' the moon!
A star—at noon.
A non-descriptus in a caravan,
A private—of no corps—a northern light
In a dark lantern—Bogie in a crape—

A figure—but no shape ;
A vizor—and no knight ;
The real abstract hero of the age ;
The staple Stranger of the stage ;
A Some One made in every man's presumption,
Frankenstein's monster—but instinct with gumption ;
Another strange state captive in the north,
Constable-guarded in an iron mask—
Still let me ask,
Hast thou no silver-platter,
No door-plate, or no card—or some such matter,
To scrawl a name upon, and then cast forth ?
Thou Scottish Barmecide, feeding the hunger
Of Curiosity with airy gammon !
Thou mystery-monger,
Dealing it out like middle cut of salmon,
That people buy and can't make head or tail of it ;
(Howbeit that puzzle never hurts the sale of it ;)
Thou chief of authors mystic and abstractical,
That lay their proper bodies on the shelf—
Keeping thyself so truly to thyself,
Thou Zimmerman made practical !
Thou secret fountain of a Scottish style,
That, like the Nile,
Hideth its source wherever it is bred,
But still keeps disemboguing
(Not disembroguing)
Thro' such broad sandy mouths without a head !
Thou disembodied author—not yet dead—

The whole world's literary Absentee!
Ah! wherefore hast thou fled,
Thou learned Nemo—wise to a degree,
Anonymous LL. D.!

Thou nameless captain of the nameless gang
That do—and inquests cannot say who did it!
Wert thou at Mrs. Donatty's death-pang?
Hast thou made gravy of Weare's watch—or hid it?
Hast thou a Blue-Beard chamber? Heaven forbid it!
I should be very loth to see thee hang!
I hope thou hast an alibi well planned,
An innocent, altho' an ink-black hand.
Tho' thou hast newly turned thy private bolt on
The curiosity of all invaders—
I hope thou art merely closeted with Colton,
Who knows a little of the *Holy Land*,
Writing thy next new novel—The Crusaders!

Perhaps thou wert even born
To be Unknown.—Perhaps hung, some foggy morn,
At Captain Coram's charitable wicket,
Pinned to a ticket
That Fate had made illegible, foreseeing
The future great unmentionable being.—

Perhaps thou hast ridden
A scholar poor on St. Augustine's Back,
Like Chatterton, and found a dusty pack
Of Rowley novels in an old chest hidden;
A little hoard of clever simulation,
That took the town—and Constable has bidden
Some hundred pounds for a continuation—
To keep and clothe thee in genteel starvation.

I liked thy Waverley—first of thy breeding;
I liked its modest "sixty years ago,"
As if it was not meant for ages' reading.
I don't like Ivanhoe,
Tho' Dymoke does—it makes him think of clattering
In iron overalls before the king,
Secure from battering, to ladies flattering,
Tuning his challenge to the gauntlet's ring—
Oh better far than all that anvil clang
It was to hear thee touch the famous string
Of Robin Hood's tough bow and make it twang,
Rousing him up, all verdant, with his clan,
Like Sagittarian Pan!

I like Guy Mannering—but not that sham son
Of Brown.—I like that literary Sampson,
Nine-tenths a Dyer, with a smack of Porson.
I like Dirk Hatteraick, that rough sea Orson
That slew the Gauger;
And Dandie Dinmont, like old Ursa Major;

And Merrilies, young Bertram's old defender,
That Scottish Witch of Endor,
That doomed thy fame. She was the Witch, I take it,
To tell a great man's fortune—or to make it!

I like thy Antiquary. With his fit on,
He makes me think of Mr. Britton,
Who has—or had—within his garden wall,
A *miniature Stone Henge*, so very small
The sparrows find it difficult to sit on;
And Dousterswivel, like Poyais' M'Gregor;
And Edie Ochiltree, that old *Blue Beggar*,
Painted so cleverly,
I think thou surely knowest Mrs. Beverly!
I like thy Barber—him that fired the *Beacon*—
But that 's a tender subject now to speak on!

I like long-armed Rob Roy.—His very charms
Fashioned him for renown!—In sad sincerity,
The man that robs or writes must have long arms,
If he 's to hand his deeds down to posterity!
Witness Miss Biffin's posthumous prosperity,
Her poor brown crumpled mummy (nothing more)
Bearing the name she bore,
A thing Time's tooth is tempted to destroy!
But Roys can never die—why else, in verity,
Is Paris echoing with "Vive le *Roy!*"
Ay, Rob shall live again, and deathless Di

Vernon, of course, shall often live again—
Whilst there 's a stone in Newgate, or a chain,
Who can pass by
Nor feel the Thief's in prison and at hand?
There be Old Bailey Jarvys on the stand!

I like thy Landlord's Tales!—I like that Idol
Of love and Lammermoor—the blue-eyed maid
That led to church the mounted cavalcade,
And then pulled up with such a bloody bridal!
Throwing equestrian Hymen on his haunches—
I like the family (not silver) branches
That hold the tapers
To light the serious legend of Montrose.—
I like M'Aulay's second-sighted vapors,
As if he could not walk or talk alone,
Without the Devil—or the Great Unknown—
Dalgetty is the dearest of Ducrows!

I like St. Leonard's Lily—drenched with dew!
I like thy Vision of the Covenanters,
That bloody-minded Graham shot and slew.
I like the battle lost and won;
The hurly burly 's bravely done,
The warlike gallops and the warlike canters!
I like that girded chieftain of the ranters,
Ready to preach down heathens, or to grapple,
With one eye on his sword,
And one upon the Word—
How *he* would cram the Caledonian Chapel!

I like stern Claverhouse, though he doth dapple
  His raven steed with blood of many a corse—
I like dear Mrs. Headrigg, that unravels
  Her texts of Scripture on a trotting horse—
She is so like Rae Wilson when he travels!

I like thy Kenilworth—but I 'm not going
  To take a Retrospective Re-Review
Of all thy dainty novels—merely showing
  The old familiar faces of a few,
      The question to renew,
How thou canst leave such deeds without a name,
Forego the unclaimed dividends of fame,
Forego the smiles of literary houris—
Mid Lothian's trump, and Fife's shrill note of praise,
    And all the Carse of Gowrie's,
When thou might'st have thy statue in Cromarty—
  Or see thy image on Italian trays,
Betwixt Queen Caroline and Buonaparté,
  Be painted by the Titian of R. A.'s,
Or vie in sign-boards with the Royal Guelph!
  P'rhaps have thy bust set cheek by jowl with Homer's,
P'rhaps send out plaster proxies of thyself
  To other Englands with Australian roamers—
    Mayhap, in Literary Owhyhee
    Displace the native wooden gods, or be
The China-Lar of a Canadian shelf!

It is not modesty that bids thee hide—
She never wastes her blushes out of sight:
It is not to invite
The world's decision, for thy fame is tried—
And thy fair deeds are scattered far and wide,
Even royal heads are with thy readers reckoned—
From men in trencher caps to trencher scholars
In crimson collars,
And learned serjeants in the Forty-Second!
Whither by land or sea art thou not beckoned?
Mayhap exported from the Frith of Forth,
Defying distance and its dim control;
Perhaps read about Stromness, and reckoned worth
A brace of Miltons for capacious soul—
Perhaps studied in the whalers, further north,
And set above ten Shakespeares near the pole!

Oh, when thou writest by Aladdin's lamp,
With such a giant genius at command,
Forever at thy stamp,
To fill thy treasury from Fairy Land,
When haply thou might'st ask the pearly hand
Of some great British Vizier's eldest daughter,
Tho' princes sought her,
And lead her in procession hymeneal,
Oh, why dost thou remain a Beau Ideal!
Why stay, a ghost, on the Lethean Wharf,
Enveloped in Scotch mist and gloomy fogs?
Why, but because thou art some puny Dwarf,

Some hopeless Imp, like Riquet with the Tuft,
Fearing, for all thy wit, to be rebuffed,
Or bullied by our great reviewing Gogs?

What in this masking age
Maketh Unknowns so many and so shy?
What but the critic's page?
One hath a cast, he hides from the world's eye;
Another hath a wen—he won't show where;
A third has sandy hair,
A hunch upon his back, or legs awry,
Things for a vile reviewer to espy!
Another has a mangel-wurzel nose—
Finally, this is dimpled,
Like a pale crumpet face, or that is pimpled,
Things for a monthly critic to expose—
Nay, what is thy own case—that being small,
Thou choosest to be nobody at all!

Well, thou art prudent, with such puny bones—
E'en like Elshender, the mysterious elf,
That shadowy revelation of thyself—
To build thee a small hut of haunted stones—
For certainly the first pernicious man
That ever saw thee, would quickly draw thee
In some vile literary caravan—
Shown for a shilling
Would be thy killing,
Think of Crachami's miserable span!
No tinier frame the tiny spark could dwell in

Than there it fell in—
But when she felt herself a show, she tried
To shrink from the world's eye, poor dwarf! and
died!

O since it was thy fortune to be born
A dwarf on some Scotch *Inch*, and then to flinch
From all the Gog-like jostle of great men,
Still with thy small crow pen
Amuse and charm thy lonely hours forlorn—
Still Scottish story daintily adorn,
Be still a shade—and when this age is fled,
When we poor sons and daughters of reality
Are in our graves forgotten and quite dead,
And Time destroys our mottoes of morality—
The lithographic hand of Old Mortality
Shall still restore thy emblem on the stone,
A featureless death's head,
And rob Oblivion ev'n of the Unknown!

ADDRESS TO MR. DYMOKE,

THE CHAMPION OF ENGLAND.

"—— Arma Virumque cano!"—VIRGIL.

MR. DYMOKE! Sir Knight! if I may be so bold—
(I 'm a poor simple gentleman just come to town,)
Is your armor put by, like the sheep in a fold?—
Is your gauntlet ta'en up, which you lately flung down?

Are you—who *that* day rode so mailed and admired,
Now sitting at ease in a library chair?
Have you sent back to Astley the war-horse you hired,
With a cheque upon Chambers to settle the fare

What 's become of the cup? Great tin-plate worker? say?
Cup and ball is a game which some people deem fun!

Oh! *three golden balls* have n't lured you to play
Rather false, Mr. D., to all pledges but one?

How defunct is the show that was chivalry's mimic!
The breastplate—the feathers—the gallant array!
So fades, so grows dim, and so dies, Mr. Dymoke!
The day of brass breeches! as Wordsworth would say!

Perchance in some village remote, with a cot,
And a cow, and a pig, and a barn-door, and all;—
You show to the parish that peace is your lot,
And plenty—tho' absent from Westminster Hall!

And of course you turn every accoutrement now
To its separate use, that your wants may be well met;—
You toss in your breastplate your pancakes, and grow
A salad of mustard and cress in your helmet.

And you delve the fresh earth with your falchion, less bright
Since hung up in sloth from its Westminster task;—

And you bake your own bread in your tin ; and, Sir Knight,
Instead of your brow, put your beer in the casque !

How delightful to sit by your beans and your peas,
With a goblet of gooseberry gallantly clutched,
And chat of the blood that had deluged the Pleas,
And drenched the King's Bench—if the glove had been touched !

If Sir Columbine Daniel, with knightly pretensions,
Had snatched your "best doe,"—he 'd have flooded the floor ;—
Nor would even the best of his crafty inventions,
"Life Preservers," have floated him out of his gore !

Oh, you and your horse ! what a couple was there !
The man and his *backer*—to win a great fight !
Though the trumpet was loud—you 'd an undisturbed air !
And the nag snuffed the feast and the fray *sans* affright !

Yet strange was the course which the good Cato bore
When he waddled tail-wise with the cup to his stall ;—

For though his departure was at the front door,
Still he went the back way out of Westminster Hall.

He went—and 't would puzzle historians to say,
When they trust Time's conveyance to carry your *mail*—
Whether caution or courage inspired him that day,
For, though he retreated, he never turned tail.

By my life, he 's a wonderful charger!—the best!
Though not for a Parthian corps!—yet for you!—
Distinguished alike at a fray and a feast,
What a Horse for a grand Retrospective Review!

What a creature to keep a hot warrior cool
When the sun's in the face, and the shade's far aloof!—
What a *tail-piece* for Bewick!—or piebald for Poole,
To bear him in safety from Elliston's hoof!

Well; hail to Old Cato! the hero of scenes!
May Astley or age ne'er his comforts abridge;—
Oh, long may he munch Amphitheatre beans,
Well "pent up in Utica" over the Bridge!

And to you, Mr. Dymoke, Cribb's rival, I keep
  Wishing all country pleasures, the bravest and best!
And oh! when you come to the Hummums to sleep,
  May you lie "like a warrior taking his rest!"

ODE TO JOSEPH GRIMALDI, SENIOR.

> "This fellow's wise enough to play the fool,
> And to do that well craves a kind of wit."
> TWELFTH NIGHT.

JOSEPH! they say thou 'st left the stage,
  To toddle down the hill of life,
And taste the flannelled ease of age,
  Apart from pantomimic strife—
"Retired—(for Young would call it so)—
The world shut out"—in Pleasant Row!

And hast thou really washed at last
  From each white cheek the red half moon!
And all thy public Clownship cast,
  To play the Private Pantaloon?
All youth—all ages—yet to be,
Shall have a heavy miss of thee!

Thou didst not preach to make us wise—
  Thou hadst no finger in our schooling—
Thou didst not "lure us to the skies"—
  Thy simple, simple trade was—Fooling!
And yet, Heaven knows! we could—we can
Much "better spare a better man!"

Oh, had it pleased the gout to take
  The reverend Croly from the stage,
Or Southey, for our quiet's sake,
  Or Mr. Fletcher, Cupid's sage,
Or, damme! namby pamby Poole—
Or any other clown or fool!

Go, Dibdin—all that bear the name,
  Go, Byway Highway man! go! go!
Go, Skeffy—man of painted fame,
  But leave thy partner, painted Joe!
I could bear Kirby on the wane,
Or Signor Paulo with a sprain!

Had Joseph Wilfred Parkins made
  His gray hairs scarce in private peace—
Had Waithman sought a rural shade—
  Or Cobbett ta'en a turnpike lease—
Or Lisle Bowles gone to *Balaam* Hill—
I think I could be cheerful still!

Had Medwin left off, to his praise,
  Dead lion kicking, like—a friend!—

Had long, long Irving gone his ways,
  To muse on death at *Ponder's End*—
Or Lady Morgan taken leave
Of Letters—still I might not grieve!

But, Joseph—every body's Jo!—
  Is gone—and grieve I will and must!
As Hamlet did for Yorick, so
  Will I for thee, (tho' not yet dust,)
And talk as he did when he missed
The kissing-crust that he had kissed!

Ah, where is now thy rolling head!
  Thy winking, reeling, *drunken* eyes,
(As old Catullus would have said,)
  Thy oven-mouth, that swallowed pies—
Enormous hunger—monstrous drouth!
Thy pockets greedy as thy mouth!

Ah, where thy ears, so often cuffed!—
  Thy funny, flapping, filching hands!—
Thy partridge body, always stuffed
  With waifs, and strays, and contrabands!—
Thy foot—like Berkeley's *Foote*—for why?
'T was often made to wipe an eye!

Ah, where thy legs—that witty pair
  For "great wits jump"—and so did they!
Lord! how they leaped in lamp-light air!
  Capered—and bounced—and strode away!—

That years should tame the legs—alack!
I 've seen spring thro' an Almanack!

But bounds will have their bound—the shocks
  Of Time will cramp the nimblest toes;
And those that frisked in silken clocks
  May look to limp in fleecy hose—
One only—(Champion of the ring)
Could ever make his Winter—Spring!

And gout, that owns no odds between
  The toe of Czar and toe of Clown,
Will visit—but I did not mean
  To moralize, though I am grown
Thus sad—Thy going seemed to beat
A muffled drum for Fun's retreat!

And, may be—'tis no time to smother
  A sigh, when two prime wags of London,
Are gone—thou, Joseph, one—the other
  A Joe!—"sic transit gloria *Munden!*"
A third departure some insist on—
Stage-apoplexy threatens Liston!—

Nay, then, let Sleeping Beauty sleep
  With ancient "*Dozey*" to the dregs—
Let Mother Goose wear mourning deep,
  And put a hatchment o'er her eggs!
Let Farly weep—for Magic's man
Is gone—his Christmas Caliban!

Let Kemble, Forbes, and Willet rain,
  As tho' they walked behind thy bier—
For since thou wilt not play again,
  What matters—if in heaven or here!
Or in thy grave, or in thy bed!—
There 's *Quick*, might just as well be dead!

Oh, how will thy departure cloud
  The lamp-light of the little breast!
The Christmas child will grieve aloud
  To miss his broadest friend and best—
Poor urchin! what avails to him
The cold New Monthly's *Ghost of Grimm?*

For who like thee could ever stride
  Some dozen paces to the mile!—
The motley, medley coach provide—
  Or like Joe Frankenstein compile
The *vegetable man* complete!—
A proper *Covent Garden* feat!

Oh, who like thee could ever drink,
  Or eat—swill—swallow—bolt—and choke!
Nod, weep, and hiccup—sneeze and wink?—
  Thy very yawn was quite a joke!
Tho' Joseph Junior acts not ill,
"There 's no Fool like the old Fool" still!

Joseph, farewell! dear funny Joe!
  We met with mirth—we part in pain!

For many a long, long year must go,
  Ere Fun can see thy like again—
For Nature does not keep great stores
Of perfect Clowns—that are not *Boors!*

ADDRESS TO SYLVANUS URBAN, ESQ.,

EDITOR OF THE GENTLEMAN'S MAGAZINE.

"Dost thou not suspect my years?"
MUCH ADO ABOUT NOTHING.

OH! Mr. Urban! never must *thou* lurch
  A sober age made serious drunk by thee;
Hop in thy pleasant way from church to church,
  And nurse thy little bald Biography.

Oh, my Sylvanus! what a heart is thine!
  And what a page attends thee! Long may I
Hang in demure confusion o'er each line
  That asks thy little questions with a sigh!

Old tottering years have nodded to their falls,
  Like pensioners that creep about and die;—
But thou, Old Parr of periodicals,
  Livest in monthly immortality!

How sweet!—as Byron of his infant said—
"Knowledge of objects" in thine eye to trace;
To see the mild no-meanings of thy head,
Taking a quiet nap upon thy face!

How dear through thy Obituary to roam,
And not a name of any name to catch!
To meet thy Criticism walking home,
Averse from rows, and never calling "Watch!"

Rich is thy page in soporific things—
Composing compositions—lulling men—
Faded old posies of unburied rings—
Confessions dozing from an opiate pen:—

Lives of Right Reverends that have never lived—
Deaths of good people that have really died—
Parishioners—hatched—husbanded—and wived,
Bankrupts and Abbots breaking side by side!

The sacred query—the remote response—
The march of serious minds, extremely slow—
The graver's cut at some right aged sconce,
Famous for nothing many years ago!

B. asks of C. if Milton e'er did write
"Comus," obscured beneath some Ludlow lid;—
And C., next month, an answer doth indite,
Informing B. that Mr. Milton did!

X. sends the portrait of a genuine flea,
Caught upon Martin Luther years agone;
And Mr. Parkes, of Shrewsbury, draws a bee,
Long dead, that gathered honey for King John.

There is no end of thee—there is no end,
Sylvanus, of thy A, B, C, D-merits!
Thou dost, with alphabets, old walls attend,
And poke the letters into holes, like ferrets!

Go on, Sylvanus!—Bear a wary eye,
The churches cannot yet be quite run out!
Some parishes must yet have been passed by—
There 's Bullock-Smithy has a church no doubt!

Go on—and close the eyes of distant ages!
Nourish the names of the undoubted dead!
So Epicures shall pick thy lobster-pages,
Heavy and lively, though but seldom *red.*

Go on! and thrive! Demurest of odd fellows!
Bottling up dulness in an ancient binn!
Still live! still prose! continue still to tell us
Old truths! no strangers, though we take them
in!

AN ADDRESS TO THE STEAM WASHING COMPANY.

" *Archer.* How many are there, *Scrub?*
Scrub. Five and forty, Sir."—BEAUX STRATAGEM.

" For shame—let the linen alone!"—
MERRY WIVES OF WINDSOR.

MR. SCRUB—Mr. Slop—or whoever you be!
The Cock of Steam Laundries—the head Patentee
Of Associate Cleansers—Chief founder and prime
Of the firm for the wholesale distilling of grime—
Copartners and dealers, in linen's propriety—
That make washing public—and wash in society—
O lend me your ear! if that ear can forego,
For a moment, the music that bubbles below—
From your new Surrey Geysers all foaming and hot—
That soft "*simmer's* sang" so endeared to the Scot—
If your hands may stand still, or your steam without danger—
If your suds will not cool, and a mere simple stranger,

Both to you and to washing, may put in a rub—
O wipe out your Amazon arms from the tub—
And lend me your ear—Let me modestly plead
For a race that your labors may soon supersede—
For a race that, now washing no living affords—
Like Grimaldi must leave their aquatic old boards,
Not with pence in their pockets to keep them at ease,
Not with bread in the funds—or investments of cheese—
But to droop like sad willows that lived by a stream,
Which the sun has sucked up into vapor and steam.
Ah, look at the Laundress, before you begrudge
Her hard daily bread to that laudable drudge—
When chanticleer singeth his earliest matins,
She slips her amphibious feet in her pattens,
And beginneth her toil while the morn is still gray,
As if she was washing the night into day—
Not with sleeker or rosier fingers Aurora
Beginneth to scatter the dew-drops before her;
Not Venus that rose from the billow so early,
Looked down on the foam with a forehead more *pearly*—
Her head is involved in an aërial mist,
And a bright-beaded bracelet encircles her wrist;

Her visage glows warm with the ardor of duty ;
She 's Industry's moral—she 's all moral beauty !
Growing brighter and brighter at every rub—
Would any man ruin her ?—No, Mr. Scrub !
No man that is manly would work her mishap—
No man that is manly would covet her cap—
Nor her apron—her hose—nor her gown made of stuff—
Nor her gin—nor her tea—nor her wet pinch of snuff !
Alas ! so *she* thought—but that slippery hope
Has betrayed her—as tho' she had trod on her soap !
And she—whose support—like the fishes that fly,
Was to have her fins wet, must now drop from her sky—
She whose living it was, and a part of her fare,
To be damped once a day, like the great white sea bear,
With her hands like a sponge, and her head like a mop—
Quite a living absorbent that revelled in slop—
She that paddled in water, must walk upon sand,
And sigh for her deeps like a turtle on land !

Lo, then, the poor Laundress, all wretched she stands,
Instead of a counterpane, wringing her hands !
All haggard and pinched, going down in life's vale,
With no fagot for burning, like Allan-a-dale !

No smoke from her flue—and no steam from her
pane,
There once she watched heaven, fearing God and
the rain—
Or gazed o'er her bleach-field so fairly engrossed,
Till the lines wandered idle from pillar to post!
Ah, where are the playful young pinners—ah,
where
The harlequin quilts that cut capers in air—
The brisk waltzing stockings—the white and the
black,
That danced on the tight-rope, or swung on the
slack—
The light sylph-like garments, so tenderly pinned,
That blew into shape, and embodied the wind!
There was white on the grass—there was white
on the spray—
Her garden—it looked like a garden of May!
But now all is dark—not a shirt 's on a shrub—
You 've ruined her prospects in life, Mr. Scrub!
You've ruined her custom—now families drop
her—
From her silver reduced—nay, reduced from her
copper!
The last of her washing is done at her eye,
One poor little kerchief that never gets dry!
From mere lack of linen she can't lay a cloth,
And boils neither barley nor alkaline broth—
But her children come round her as victuals grow
scant,

And recall, with foul faces, the source of theii
want—
When she thinks of their poor little mouths to be
fed,
And then thinks of her trade that is utterly dead,
And even its pearlashes laid in the grave—
Whilst her tub is a dry rotting, stave after stave,
And the greatest of Coopers, ev'n he that they
dub
Sir Astley, can't bind up her heart or her tub—
Need you wonder she curses your bones, Mr.
Scrub?
Need you wonder, when steam has deprived her
of bread,
If she prays that the evil may visit *your* head—
Nay, scald all the heads of your Washing Com-
mittee—
If she wishes you all the soot blacks of the city—
In short, not to mention all plagues without num-
ber,
If she wishes you all in the *Wash* at the Hum-
ber!

Ah, perhaps, in some moment of drouth and
despair,
When her linen got scarce, and her washing grew
rare—
When the sum of her suds might be summed in a
bowl,
And the rusty cold iron quite entered her soul—

When, perhaps, the last glance of her wandering
eye
Had caught "the Cock Laundresses' Coach" going
by,
Or her lines that hung idle, to waste the fine
weather,
And she thought of her wrongs and her rights
both together,
In a lather of passion that frothed as it rose,
Too angry for grammar, too lofty for prose,
On her sheet—if a sheet were still left her—to
write,
Some remonstrance like this then, perchance, saw
the light—

LETTER OF REMONSTRANCE FROM BRIDGET JONES

TO THE NOBLEMEN AND GENTLEMEN FORMING THE WASHING COMMITTEE.

It 's a shame, so it is—men can't Let alone
Jobs as is Woman's right to do—and go about
there Own—
Theirs Reforms enuff Alreddy without your new
schools
For washing to sit Up—and push the Old Tubs
from their stools!
But your just like the Raddicals—for upsetting of
the Sudds

When the world wagged well enuff—and Wommen washed your old dirty duds,
I 'm Certain sure Enuff your Ann Sisters had no steem Indians, that 's Flat—
But I warrant your Four Fathers went as Tidy and gentlemanny for all that—
I suppose your the Family as lived in the Great Kittle
I see on Clapham Commun, some times a very considerable period back when I were little,
And they Said it went with Steem—But that was a joke!
For I never see none come of it—that 's out of it —but only sum Smoak—
And for All your Power of Horses about your Indians you never had but Two
In my time to draw you About to Fairs—and hang you, you know that 's true!
And for All your fine Perspectuses—howsomever you bewhich 'em,
Theirs as Pretty ones off Primerows Hill, as ever a one at Mitchum,
Thof I cant sea What Prospectives and washing has with one another to Do—
It ant as if a Bird'seye Hankicher could take a Birdshigh view!
But Thats your look out—I 've not much to do with that—But pleas God to hold up fine,
Id show you caps and pinners and small things as lilliwhit as Ever crosst the Line

Without going any Father off then Little Parodies Place,
And Thats more than you Can—and Ill say it behind your face—
But when Folks talks of washing, it ant for you to Speak—
As kept Dockter Pattyson out of his Shirt for a Weak!
Thinks I, when I heard it—Well, there 's a pretty go!
That comes o' not marking of things or washing out the marks, and Huddling 'em up so!
Till Their friends comes and owns them, like drownded corpeses in a Vault,
But may Hap you havint Larned to spel—and That ant your Fault,
Only you ought to leafe the Linnins to them as has Larned—
For if it warnt for Washing—and whare Bills is concarned
What 's the Yuse, of all the world, for a Wommans Headication,
And Their Being maid Schollards of Sundays—fit for any Cityation.

Well, what I says is This—when every Kittle has its spout,
Theirs no nead for Companys to puff steem about!
To be sure its very Well, when Their ant enuff Wind

For blowing up Boats with—but not to hurt human kind
Like that Pearkins with his Blunderbush, that 's loaded with hot water,
Thof a X Sherrif might know Better, than make things for slaughtter,
As if War warnt Cruel enuff—wherever it befalls,
Without shooting poor sogers, with sich scalding hot balls—
But thats not so Bad as a Sett of Bear Faced Scrubbs
As joins their Sopes together, and sits up Steem rubbing Clubs,
For washing Dirt Cheap—and eating other Peple's grubs!
Which is all verry Fine for you and your Patent Tea,
But I wonders How Poor Wommen is to get Their Beau-He!
They must drink Hunt wash (the only wash God nose there will be!)
And their Little drop of Somethings as they takes for their Goods,
When you and your Steem has ruined (G—d forgive mee) their lively Hoods,
Poor Wommen as was born to Washing in their youth!
And now must go and Larn other Buisnesses Four Sooth!
But if so be they They leave their Lines what are they to go at—

They won't do for Angell's—nor any Trade like
That,
Nor we cant Sow Babby Work—for that 's all
Bespoke—
For the Queakers in Bridle ! and a vast of the
confined Folk
Do their own of Themselves—even the bettermost
of em—aye, and evn them of middling de-
grees—
Why Lauk help you Babby Linen ant Bread and
Cheese !
Nor we can't go a hammering the roads into Dust,
But we must all go and be Bankers—like Mr.
Marshes and Mr. Chamberses—and that 's
what we must !
God nose you oght to have more Concern for our
Sects,
When you nose you have sucked us and hanged
round our Mutherly necks,
And remembers what you Owes to Wommen
Besides washing—
You ant, blame you ! like Men to go a slushing
and sloshing
In mop caps, and pattins, adoing of Females La-
bers
And prettily jeared At you great Horse God
Meril things, ant you now by your next
door naybors—
Lawk I thinks I see you with your Sleaves tuckt
up

No more like Washing than is drownding of a Pupp,
And for all Your Fine Water Works going round and round
They 'll scruntch your Bones some day—I 'll be bound
And no more nor be a gudgement—for it cant come to good
To sit up agin Providince, which your a doing—nor not fit It should,
For man warnt maid for Wommens starvation,
Nor to do away Laundrisses as is Links of the Creation—
And cant be dun without in any Country But a naked Hottinpot Nation.
Ah, I wish our Minister would take one of your Tubbs
And preach a Sermon in it, and give you some good rubs—
But I warrants you reads (for you cant spel we nose) nyther Bybills or Good Tracks,
Or youd no better than Taking the close off one's Backs—
And let your neighbors oxin an Asses alone—
And every Thing thats hern—and give every one their Hone!

Well, its God for us Al, and every Washer Wommen for herself,
And so you might, without shoving any on us off the shelf,

But if you warnt Noddis you Let wommen abe
And pull of Your Pattins—and leave the washing to we
That nose what 's what—Or mark what I say,
Youl make a fine Kittle of fish of Your Close some Day—
When the Aulder men wants Their Bibs and their ant nun at all,
And Cris mass cum—and never a Cloth to lay in Gild Hall,
Or send a damp shirt to his Woship the Mare
Till hes rumatiz Poor Man, and cant set uprite to do good in his Harm-Chare—
Besides Miss-Matching Larned Ladys Hose, as is sent for you not to wash (for you dont wash) but to stew
And make Peples Stockins yeller as oght to be Blew
With a vast more like That—and all along of Steem
Which warnt meand by Nater for any sich skeam—
But thats your Losses and youl have to make It Good,
And I cant say I'm Sorry afore God if you shoud,
For men mought Get their Bread a great many ways
Without taking ourn—aye, and Moor to your Prays

You might go and skim the creme off Mr. Muck-
Adam's milky ways—that 's what you might,
Or bete Carpets—or get into Parleamint—or drive
Crabrolays from morning to night,
Or, if you must be of our sects, be Watchmen,
and slepe upon a poste!
(Which is an od way of sleping, I must say—and
a very hard pillow at most,)
Or you might be any trade, as we are not on that
I 'm awares,
Or be Watermen now, (not Water-wommen) and
roe peple up and down Hungerford stares,
Or if You Was even to Turn Dust Men a *dry
sifting* Dirt!
But you oughtint to Hurt Them as never Did You
no Hurt!

Yourn with Anymocity,

BRIDGET JONES.

ODE TO CAPTAIN PARRY.

"By the North Pole, I do challenge thee!"
LOVE'S LABORS LOST.

PARRY, my man! has thy brave leg
Yet struck its foot against the peg
  On which the world is spun?
Or hast thou found No Thoroughfare
Writ by the hand of Nature there
  Where man has never run!

Hast thou yet traced the Great Unknown
Of channels in the Frozen Zone,
  Or held at Icy Bay,
Hast thou still missed the proper track
For homeward Indiamen that lack
  A bracing by the way?

Still hast thou wasted toil and trouble
On nothing but the North-Sea Bubble
  Of geographic scholar?
Or found new ways for ships to shape,
Instead of winding round the Cape,
  A short cut thro' the collar!

Hast found the way that sighs were sent to[1]
The Pole—tho' God knows whom they went to!
That track revealed to Pope—
Or if the Arctic waters sally,
Or terminate in some blind alley,
A chilly path to grope?

Alas! tho' Ross, in love with snows,
Has painted them *couleur de rose*,
It is a dismal doom,
As Claudio saith, to winter thrice,
"In regions of thick-ribbed ice"—
All bright—and yet all gloom!

'Tis well for Gheber souls that sit
Before the fire and worship it
With pecks of Wallsend coals,
With feet upon the fender's front,
Roasting their corns—like Mr. Hunt—
To speculate on poles.

'Tis easy for our Naval Board—
'Tis easy for our Civic Lord
Of London and of ease,
That lies in ninety feet of down,
With fur on his nocturnal gown,
To talk of Frozen Seas!

1 "And waft a sigh from Indus to the Pole."
Eloisa to Abelard.

'Tis fine for Monsieur Ude to sit,
And prate about the mundane spit,
  And babble of *Cook's* track—
He 'd roast the leather off his toes,
Ere he would trudge thro' polar snows,
  To plant a British *Jack!*

Oh, not the proud licentious great,
That travel on a carpet skate,
  Can value toils like thine!
What 'tis to take a Hecla range,
Through ice unknown to Mrs. Grange,
  And alpine lumps of brine!

But we, that mount the Hill o' Rhyme,
Can tell how hard it is to climb
  The lofty slippery steep.
Ah! there are more Snow Hills than that
Which doth black Newgate, like a hat,
  Upon its forehead keep.

Perchance thou 'rt now—while I am writing—
Feeling a bear's wet grinder biting
  About thy frozen spine!
Or thou thyself art eating whale,
Oily, and underdone, and stale,
  That, haply, crossed thy line!

But I 'll not dream such dreams of ill—
Rather will I believe thee still

Safe cellared in the snow—
Reciting many a gallant story,
Of British kings and British glory,
To crony Esquimaux—

Cheering that dismal game where Night
Makes one slow move from black to white
Thro' all the tedious year—
Or smitten by some fond frost fair,
That combed out crystals from her hair,
Wooing a seal-skin Dear!

So much a long communion tends,
As Byron says, to make us friends
With what we daily view—
God knows the daintiest taste may come
To love a nose that's like a plum
In marble, cold and blue!

To dote on hair, an oily fleece!
As tho' it hung from Helen o' Greece—
They say that love prevails
Ev'n in the veriest polar land—
And surely she may steal thy hand
That used to steal thy nails!

But ah, ere thou art fixt to marry,
And take a polar Mrs. Parry,
Think of a six months' gloom—
Think of the wintry waste, and hers,

Each furnished with a dozen *furs*,
  Think of thine icy *dome!*

Think of the children born to *blubber!*
Ah me! hast thou an Indian rubber
  Inside!—to hold a meal
For months—about a stone and half
Of whale, and part of a sea calf—
  A fillet of salt veal!—

Some walrus ham—no trifle but
A decent steak—a solid cut
  Of seal—no wafer slice!
A reindeer's tongue and drink beside!
Gallons of Sperm—not rectified!
  And pails of water-ice!

Oh, canst thou fast and then feast thus?
Still come away, and teach to us
  Those blessed altenations—
To-day to run our dinners fine,
To feed on air and then to dine
  With Civic Corporations—

To save th' Old Bailey daily shilling,
And then to take a half year's filling
  In P. N.'s pious Row—
When asked to Hock and haunch o' ven'son,
Thro' something we have worn our pens on
  For Longman and his Co.

O come and tell us what the Pole is—
Whether it singular and sole is—
  Or straight, or crooked bent—
If very thick or very thin—
Made of what wood—and if akin
  To those there be in Kent.

There 's Combe, there 's Spurzheim, and there 's
    Gall,
Have talked of poles—yet, after all,
  What has the public learned?
And Hunt's account must still defer—
He sought the *poll* at Westminster—
  And is not yet *returned!*

Alvanly asks if whist, dear soul,
Is played in snow-storms near the Pole,
  And how the fur-man deals?
And Eldon doubts if it be true,
That icy Chancellors really do
  Exist upon the *seals!*

Barrow, by well-fed office grates,
Talks of his own bechristened Straits,
  And longs that he were there;
And Croker, in his cabriolet,
Sighs o'er his brown horse, at his Bay,
  And pants to cross the *mer!*

O come away, and set us right,
And, haply, throw a northern light

On questions such as these :—
Whether, when this drowned world was lost,
The surflux waves were locked in frost,
And turned to Icy Seas!

Is Ursa Major white or black?
Or do the Polar tribes attack
Their neighbors—and what for?
Whether they ever play at cuffs,
And then, if they take off their muffs
In pugilistic war?

Tell us, is *Winter* champion there,
As in our milder fighting air?
Say, what are *Chilly* loans?
What cures they have for rheums beside,
And if their hearts gets ossified
From eating bread of bones?

Whether they are such dwarfs—the quicker
To circulate the vital liquor—
And then, from head to heel—
How short the Methodists must choose
Their dumpy envoys not to lose
Their toes in spite of zeal?

Whether 't will soften or sublime it
To preach of Hell in such a climate—
Whether may Wesley hope
To win their souls—or that old function

Of seals—with the extreme of unction—
  Bespeaks them for the Pope?

Whether the lamps will e'er be "learned"
Where six months' "midnight oil" is burned,
  Or Letters must defer
With people that have never conned
An A, B, C, but live beyond
  The *Sound of Lancaster!*

O come away at any rate—
Well hast thou earned a downier state—
  With all thy hardy peers—
Good lack, thou must be glad to smell dock,
And rub thy feet with opodeldock,
  After such frosty years.

Mayhap, some gentle dame at last,
Smit by the perils thou hast passed,
  However coy before,
Shall bid thee now set up thy rest
In that *Brest Harbor*, Woman's breast,
  And tempt the Fates no more.

ADDRESS TO R. W. ELLISTON, ESQUIRE,

THE GREAT LESSEE!

" Do you know, you villain, that I am at this moment the greatest man living?" WILD OATS.

OH! Great Lessee! Great Manager! Great Man!
Oh, Lord High Elliston! Immortal Pan
Of all the pipes that play in Drury Lane!
Macready's master! Westminster's high *Dane!*
(As Galway Martin, in the House's walls,
Hamlet and Doctor Ireland justly calls!)
Friend to the sweet and ever-smiling Spring!
Magician of the lamp and prompter's ring!
Drury's Aladdin! Whipper-in of Actors!
Kicker of rebel-preface-malefactors!
Glass-blowers' corrector! King of the cheque-
taker!
At once Great Leamington and Winston-Maker!
Dramatic Bolter of plain *Bunns* and Cakes!
In silken *hose* the most reformed of *Rakes!*
Oh, Lord High Elliston! lend me an ear!
(Poole is away, and Williams shall keep clear)

While I, in little slips of prose, not verse,
Thy splendid course, as pattern-worker, rehearse!

Bright was thy youth—thy manhood brighter still—
The greatest Romeo upon Holborn Hill—
Lightest comedian of the pleasant day,
When Jordan threw her sunshine o'er a play!
When fair Thalia held a merry reign,
And Wit was at her Court in Drury Lane!
Before the day when Authors wrote, of course,
The "Entertainment *not* for Man but Horse."
Yet these, though happy, were but subject times,
And no man cares for bottom-steps that climbs—
Far from my wish it is to stifle down
The hours that saw thee snatch the Surrey crown!
Tho' now thy hand a mightier sceptre wields,
Fair was thy reign in sweet St. George's Fields.
Dibdin was *Premier*—and a golden *age*
For a short time enriched the subject stage.
Thou hadst, than other Kings, more peace-and-plenty;
Ours but one Bench could boast, whilst thou hadst twenty;
But the times changed—and Booth-acting no more
Drew Rulers' shillings to the gallery-door.
Thou didst, with bag and baggage, wander thence,
Repentant, like thy neighbor Magdalens!

Next, the Olympic Games were tried, each feat
Practised, the most bewitching in Wych Street.
Rochester there in dirty ways again
Revelled—and lived once more in Drury Lane:
But thou, R. W.! kept'st thy moral ways,
Pit-lecturing 'twixt the farces and the plays,
A lamplight Irving to the butcher boys
That soiled the benches and that made a noise:—
Rebuking—Half a Robert, Half a Charles—
The well-billed Man that called for promised Carles;
"Sir!—Have you yet to know! Hush—hear me out!
A Man—pray silence!—may be down with gout,
Or want—or Sir—aw!—listen!—may be fated,
Being in debt, to be incarcerated!
You—in the back!—can scarcely hear a line!
Down from those benches—butchers—they are *mine!*"

Lastly—and thou wert built for it by nature!—
Crowned was thy head in Drury Lane The*a*tre!
Gentle George Robins saw that it was good,
And Renters clucked around thee in a brood.
King thou wert made of Drury and of Kean!
Of many a lady and of many a Quean!
With Poole and Larpent was thy reign begun—
But now thou turnest from the Dead and Dun,
Hook's in thine eye, to write thy plays, no doubt,
And Colman lives to cut the damnlets out!

Oh, worthy of the house! the King's commission!
Is n't thy condition "a most blessed condition?"
Thou reignest over Winston, Kean, and all,
The very lofty and the very small—
Showest the plumbless Bunn the way to kick—
Keepest a Williams for thy veriest stick—
Seest a Vestris in her sweetest moments,
Without the danger of newspaper comments—
Tellest Macready, as none dared before,
Thine open mind from the half-open door!—
(Alas! I fear he has left Melpomene's crown,
To be a Boniface in Buxton town!)—
Thou holdst the watch, as half-price people know,
And callest to them, to a moment—"Go!"
Teachest the sapient Sapio how to sing—
Hangest a cat most oddly by the wing—
(To prove, no doubt, the endless free list ended,
And all, except the public press, suspended,)
Hast known the length of a Cubitt-foot—and kissed
The pearly whiteness of a Stephens' wrist—
Kissing and pitying—tender and humane!
"By Heaven she loves me! Oh, it is too plain!"
A sigh like this thy trembling passion slips,
Dimpling the warm Madeira at thy lips!

Go on, Lessee! Go on, and prosper well!
Fear not, though forty Glass-blowers should rebel—

Show them how thou hast long befriended them,
And teach Dubois their treason to condemn!
Go on! addressing pits in prose and worse!
Be long, be slow, be any thing but terse—
Kiss to the gallery the hand that 's gloved—
Make Bunn the Great, and Winston the Beloved,
Ask the two shilling Gods for leave to dun
With words the cheaper Deities in the *One!*
Kick Mr. Poole unseen from scene to scene,
Cane Williams still, and stick to Mr. Kean,
Warn from the benches all the rabble rout;
Say, those are *mine*—"In parliament, or out!"
Swing cats—for in thy house there 's surely space—
O Beasley, for such pastime, planned the place!
Do any thing!—Thy fame, thy fortune, nourish!
Laugh and grow fat! be eloquent, and flourish!
Go on—and but in this reverse the thing,
Walk backward with wax lights before the King—
Go on! Spring ever in thine eye! Go on!
Hope's favorite child! ethereal Elliston!

ADDRESS TO MARIA DARLINGTON,

ON HER RETURN TO THE STAGE.

"It was Maria!—

And better fate did Maria deserve than to have her banns forbid——

She had, since that, she told me, strayed as far as Rome, and walked round St. Peter's once—and returned back——"

See the whole Story, in Sterne and the Newspapers.

THOU art come back again to the stage,
Quite as blooming as when thou didst leave it;
And 'tis well for this fortunate age
That thou didst not, by going off, grieve it!
It is pleasant to see thee again—
Right pleasant to see thee, by Herclé,
Unmolested by pea-colored Hayne!
And free from that thou-and-thee Berkeley!

Thy sweet foot, my Foote, is as light
(Not *my* Foote—I speak by correction)
As the snow on some mountain at night,
Or the snow that has long on thy neck shone.
The pit is in raptures to free thee,

The Boxes impatient to greet thee,
The Galleries quite clam'rous to see thee,
And thy scenic relations to meet thee!

Ah, where was thy sacred retreat?
Maria! ah, where hast thou been,
With thy two little wandering feet,
Far away from all peace and pea-green!
Far away from Fitzhardinge the bold,
Far away from himself and his lot!
I envy the place thou hast strolled,
If a stroller thou art—which thou 'rt not!

Sterne met thee, poor wandering thing,
Methinks, at the close of the day—
When thy Billy had just slipped his string,
And thy little dog quite gone astray—
He bade thee to sorrow no more—
He wished thee to lull thy distress
In his bosom—he could n't do more,
And a Christian could hardly do less!

Ah, me! for thy small plaintive pipe,
I fear we must look at thine eye—
I would it were my task to wipe
That hazel orb thoroughly dry!
Oh sure 'tis a barbarous deed
To give pain to the feminine mind—
But the wooer that left thee to bleed
Was a creature more killing than kind!

The man that could tread on a worm
  Were a brute—and inhuman to boot;
But he merits a much harsher term
  That can wantonly tread on a Foote!
Soft mercy and gentleness blend
  To make up a Quaker—but he
That spurned thee could scarce be a *Friend*,
  Tho' he dealt in that Thou-ing of thee!

They that loved thee, Maria, have flown!
  The friends of the midsummer hour!
But those friends now in anguish atone,
  And mourn o'er thy desolate bower.
Friend Hayne, the Green Man, is quite out,
  Yea, utterly out of his bias;
And the faithful Fitzhardinge, no doubt,
  Is counting his Ave Marias!

Ah, where wert thou driven away,
  To feast on thy desolate woe?
We have witnessed thy weeping in play,
  But none saw the earnest tears flow—
Perchance thou wert truly forlorn—
  Tho' none but the fairies could mark
Where they hung upon some Berkeley thorn,
  Or the thistles in Burderop Park!

Ah, perhaps, when old age's white snow
  Has silvered the crown of Hayne's nob—
For even the greenest will grow

As hoary as "Whiteheaded Bob"—
He 'll wish, in the days of his prime,
He had been rather kinder to one
He hath left to the malice of Time—
A woman—so weak and undone!

ODE TO W. KITCHENER, M.D.

AUTHOR OF THE COOK'S ORACLE—OBSERVATIONS ON VOCAL MUSIC—THE ART OF INVIGORATING AND PROLONGING LIFE—PRACTICAL OBSERVATIONS ON TELESCOPES, OPERA GLASSES, AND SPECTACLES—THE HOUSEKEEPER'S LEDGER—AND THE PLEASURE OF MAKING A WILL.

"I rule the roast, as Milton says!"—CALEB QUOTEM.

Oh! multifarious man!
Thou Wondrous, Admirable Kitchen Crichton!
Born to enlighten
The laws of Optics, Peptics, Music, Cooking—
Master of the Piano—and the Pan—
As busy with the kitchen as the skies!
Now looking
At some rich stew thro' Galileo's eyes—
Or boiling eggs—timed to a metronome—
As much at home

In spectacles as in mere isinglass—
In the art of frying brown—as a digression
On music and poetical expression—
Whereas, how few of all our cooks, alas!
Could tell Calliope from "Callipee!"
How few there be
Could leave the lowest for the highest stories,
(Observatories,)
And turn, like thee, Diana's calculator,
However *cook's* synonymous with *Kater!* [1]
Alas! still let me say,
How few could lay
The carving knife beside the tuning-fork,
Like the proverbial *Jack* ready for any work!

Oh, to behold thy features in thy book!
Thy proper head and shoulders in a plate,
How it would look!
With one raised eye watching the dial's date,
And one upon the roast, gently cast down—
Thy chops—done nicely brown—
The garnished brow—with "a few leaves of bay"—
The hair—"done Wiggy's way!"
And still one studious finger near thy brains,
As if thou wert just come
From editing some
New soup—or hashing Dibdin's cold remains!

[1] Captain Kater, the Moon's Surveyor.

Or, Orpheus-like—fresh from thy dying strains
Of music—Epping luxuries of sound,
As Milton says, "in many a bout
Of linked sweetness long drawn out,"
Whilst all thy tame stuffed leopards listened round!

Oh, rather thy whole proper length reveal,
Standing like Fortune—on the jack—thy wheel.
(Thou art, like Fortune, full of chops and changes,
Thou hast a fillet too before thine eye!)
Scanning our kitchen and our vocal ranges,
As tho' it were the same to sing or fry—
Nay, so it is—hear how Miss Paton's throat
Makes "fritters" of a note!
And how Tom Cook (Fryer and Singer born
By name and nature) oh! how night and morn
He for the nicest public taste doth dish
up
The good things from that *Pan* of music, Bishop!
And is not reading near akin to feeding,
Or why should *Oxford Sausages* be fit
Receptacles for wit?
Or why should Cambridge put its little, smart,
Minced brains into a *Tart?*
Nay, then, thou wert but wise to frame receipts,
Book-treats,
Equally to instruct the Cook and cram her—
Receipts to be devoured, as well as read,
The Culinary Art in gingerbread—
The Kitchen's *Eaten* Grammar!

Oh, very pleasant is thy motley page—
Ay, very pleasant in its chatty vein—
So—in a kitchen—would have talked Montaigne,
That merry Gascon—humorist, and sage!
Let slender minds with single themes engage,
Like Mr. Bowles with his eternal Pope—
Or Haydon on perpetual Haydon—or
Hume on "Twice three make four,"
Or Lovelass upon Wills—Thou goest on
Plaiting ten topics, like Tate Wilkinson!
Thy brain is like a rich Kaleidoscope,
Stuffed with a brilliant medley of odd bits,
And ever shifting on from change to change,
Saucepans—old Songs—Pills—Spectacles—and Spits!
Thy range is wider than a Rumford Range!
Thy grasp a miracle!—till I recall
Th' indubitable cause of thy variety—
Thou art, of course, th' Epitome of all
That spying—frying—singing—mixed Society
Of Scientific Friends, who used to meet
Welch Rabbits—and thyself—in Warren Street!

Oh, hast thou still those Conversazioni,
Where learned visitors discoursed—and fed?
There came Belzoni,
Fresh from the ashes of Egyptian dead—
And gentle Poki—and that Royal Pair,
Of whom thou didst declare—

"Thauks to the greatest *Cooke* we ever read—
They were—what *Sandwiches* should be—half
bred!"
There famed M'Adam from his manual toil
Relaxed—and freely owned he took thy hints
On "making *Broth* with *Flints*"—
There Parry came, and showed thee polar oil
For melted butter—Combe with his medullary
Notions about the *Skullery*,
And Mr. Poole, too partial to a broil—
There witty Rogers came, that punning elf!
Who used to swear thy book
Would really look
A *Delphic* "Oracle," if laid on *Delf*—
There, once a month, came Campbell and discussed
His own—and thy own—"*Magazine* of *Taste*"—
There Wilberforce the Just
Came, in his old black suit, till once he traced
Thy sly advice to *Poachers* of Black Folks,
That "dq not break their *yolks*,"—
Which huffed him home, in grave disgust and
haste!

There came John Clare, the poet, nor forbore
Thy *Patties*—thou wert hand-and-glove with
Moore,
Who called thee "*Kitchen Addison*"—for why?
Thou givest rules for Health and Peptic Pills,
Forms for made dishes, and receipts for Wills,

"*Teaching us how to live and how to die!*"
There came thy Cousin-Cook, good Mrs. Fry—
There Trench, the Thames Projector, first brought on
His sine *Quay* non—
There Martin would drop in on Monday eves,
Or Fridays, from the pens, and raise his breath
'Gainst cattle days and death—
Answered by Mellish, feeder of fat beeves,
Who swore that Frenchmen never could be eager
For fighting on soup meagre—
"And yet (as thou would'st add,) the French have seen
A Marshal *Tureen!*"

Great was thy Evening Cluster!—often graced
With Dollond—Burgess—and Sir Humphrey Davy!
'T was there M'Dermot first inclined to Taste—
There Colburn learned the art of making paste
For puffs—and Accum analyzed a gravy,
Colman—the Cutter of Coleman Street, 'tis said
Came there—and Parkins with his Ex-wise-head,
(His claim to letters)—Kater, too, the Moon's
Crony—and Graham, lofty on balloons—
There Croly stalked with holy humor heated,
Who wrote a light horse play, which Yates completed—
And Lady Morgan, that grinding organ,

And Brasbridge telling anecdotes of spoons—
Madame Valbrèque thrice honored thee, and
came
With great Rossini, his own bow and fiddle—
The Dibdins—Tom, Charles, Frognall—came
with tuns
Of poor old books, old puns!
And even Irving spared a night from fame—
And talked—till thou didst stop him in the mid-
dle,
To serve round *Tewah-diddle!* [1]

Then all the guests rose up, and sighed good-bye!
So let them:—thou thyself art still a *Host!*
Dibdin—Cornaro—Newton—Mrs. Fry!
Mrs. Glasse, Mr. Spec!—Lovelass—and Weber,
Matthews in Quot'em—Moore's fire-worshipping
Gheber—
Thrice-worthy Worthy, seem by thee engrossed!
Howbeit the Peptic Cook still rules the roast,
Potent to hush all ventriloquial snarling—
And ease the bosom pangs of indigestion!
Thou art, sans question,
The Corporation's love—its Doctor *Darling!*
Look at the Civic Palate—nay, the bed
Which set dear Mrs. Opie on supplying
"Illustrations of *Lying!*"
Ninety square feet of down from heel to head

[1] The Doctor's composition for a *night-cap.*

It measured, and I dread
Was haunted by that terrible night *Mare*,
A monstrous burthen on the corporation!
Look at the Bill of Fare, for one day's share,
Sea-turtles by the score—Oxen by droves,
Geese, turkeys, by the flock—fishes and loaves
Countless, as when the Lilliputian nation
Was making up the huge man-mountain's ration!

Oh! worthy Doctor! surely thou hast driven
The squatting Demon from great Garratt's breast—
(His honor seemed to rest!—)
And what is thy reward?—Hath London given
Thee public thanks for thy important service?
Alas! not even
The tokens it bestowed on Howe and Jervis!—
Yet could I speak as Orators should speak
Before the worshipful the Common Council,
(Utter my bold bad grammar and pronounce ill,)
Thou should'st not miss thy Freedom, for a week,
Richly engrossed on vellum:—Reason urges
That he who rules our cookery—that he
Who edits soups and gravies, ought to be
A *Citizen*, where sauce can make a *Burgess!*

AN ADDRESS TO THE VERY REVEREND JOHN IRELAND, D.D.

CHARLES FYNES CLINTON, LL.D.
THOMAS CAUSTON, D.D.
HOWEL HOLLAND EDWARDS, M.A.
JOSEPH ALLEN, M.A.
LORD HENRY FITZROY, M.A
THE BISHOP OF EXETER.
WM. H. EDWARD BENTINCK, M.A.
JAMES WEBBER, B.D.
WILLIAM SHORT, D.D.
JAMES TOURNAY, D.D.
ANDREW BELL, D.D.
GEORGE HOLCOMBE, D.D.

THE DEAN AND CHAPTER OF WESTMINSTER.

" Sure the Guardians of the Temple can never think they get enough." CITIZEN OF THE WORLD.

OH, very reverend Dean and Chapter,
  Exhibitors of giant men,
Hail to each surplice-backed Adapter
  Of England's dead, in her Stone den!
Ye teach us properly to prize
  Two-shilling Grays, and Gays, and Handels,
And, to throw light upon our eyes,
  Deal in Wax Queens like old wax candles.

Oh, reverend showmen, rank and file,
  Call in your shillings, two and two;

March with them up the middle aisle,
  And cloister them from public view.
Yours surely are the dusty dead,
  Gladly ye look from bust to bust,
Setting a price on each great head,
  To make it come down with the dust.

Oh, as I see you walk along
  In ample sleeves and ample back
A pursy and well-ordered throng,
  Thoroughly fed, thoroughly black!
In vain I strive me to be dumb—
  You keep each bard like fatted kid,
Grind bones for bread like Fee faw fum!
  And drink from skulls as Byron did!

The profitable Abbey is
  A sacred 'Change for stony stock,
Not that a speculation 'tis—
  The profit 's founded on a rock.
Death, Dean, and Doctors, in each nave
  Bony investments have inurned!
And hard 't would be to find a grave
  From which "no money is returned!"

Here many a pensive pilgrim, brought
  By reverence for those learned bones,
Shall often come and walk your short
  Two-shilling[1] fare upon the stones.—

[1] Since this poem was written, Doctor Ireland and those in

Ye have that talisman of Wealth,
  Which puddling chemists sought of old,
Till ruined out of hope and health ;—
  The Tomb 's the stone that turns to gold !

Oh, licensed cannibals, ye eat
  Your dinners from your own dead race,
Think Gray, preserved, a " funeral meat,"
  And Dryden, deviled, after grace,
A relish ;—and you take your meal
  From Rare Ben Jonson underdone,
Or, whet your holy knives on Steele,
  To cut away at Addison !

O say, of all this famous age,
  Whose learned bones your hopes expect,
Oh have ye numbered Rydal's sage,
  Or Moore among your Ghosts elect ?
Lord Byron was not doomed to make
  You richer by his final sleep—
Why don't ye warn the Great to take
  Their ashes to no other heap ?

Southey's reversion have ye got ?
  With Coleridge, for his body, made
A bargain ?—has Sir Walter Scott,
  Like Peter Schlemihl, sold his shade ?

authority under him have reduced the fares. It is gratifying to the English People to know, that while butchers' meat is rising, tombs are falling.

Has Rogers haggled hard, or sold
  His features for your marble shows,
Or Campbell bartered, ere he 's cold,
  All interest in his " *bone* repose ? "

Rare is your show, ye righteous men !
  Priestly Politos—rare, I ween ;
But should ye not *outside* the Den
  Paint up what *in* it may be seen ?
A long green Shakespeare, with a deer
  Grasped in the many folds it died in—
A Butler stuffed from ear to ear,
  Wet White Bears weeping o'er a Dry-den !

Paint Garrick up like Mr. Paap,
  A Giant of some inches high ;
Paint Handel up, that organ chap,
  With you, as grinders, in his eye ;
Depict some plaintive antique thing,
  And say th' original may be seen ;—
Blind Milton with a dog and string
  May be the Beggar o' Bethnal Green !

Put up in Poet's Corner, near
  The little door, a platform small ;
Get there a monkey—never fear,
  You 'll catch the gapers one and all !
Stand each of ye a Body Guard,
  A Trumpet under either fin,
And yell away in Palace Yard
  "All dead ! All dead ! Walk in ! Walk in !"

(But when the people are inside,
  Their money paid—I pray you, bid
The keepers not to mount and ride
  A race around each coffin lid.—
Poor Mrs. Bodkin thought last year,
  That it was hard—the woman clacks—
To have so little in her ear—
  And be so hurried through the Wax!—)

"Walk in! two shillings only! come!
  Be not by country grumblers funked!—
Walk in, and see th' illustrious dumb!
  The Cheapest House for the defunct!"
Write up, 't will breed some just reflection,
  And every rude surmise 't will stop—
Write up, that you have no connection
  (In large)—with any other shop!

And still, to catch the Clowns the more,
  With samples of your shows in Wax,
Set some old Harry near the door
  To answer queries with his *axe*.—
Put up some general begging-trunk—
  Since the last broke by some mishap
You 've all a bit of General Monk,
  From the respect you bore his Cap!

ODE TO H. BODKIN, ESQ.,

SECRETARY TO THE SOCIETY FOR THE SUPPRESSION OF MENDICITY.

"This is your charge—you shall comprehend all vagrom men."— MUCH ADO ABOUT NOTHING.

HAIL, King of Shreds and Patches, hail,
  Disperser of the Poor!
Thou Dog in office, set to bark
  All beggars from the door!

Great overseer of overseers,
  And Dealer in old rags!
Thy public duty never fails,
  Thy ardor never flags!

Oh, when I take my walks abroad,
  How many Poor I *miss!*
Had Doctor Watts walked now-a-days
  He would have written this!

So well thy Vagrant catchers prowl,
  So clear thy caution keeps

The path—O, Bodkin, sure thou hast
  The eye that never sleeps!

No Belisarius pleads for alms,
  No Benbow lacketh legs;
The pious man in black is now
  The only man that begs!

Street-Handels are disorganized,
  Disbanded every band!—
The silent *scraper* at the door
  Is scarce allowed to stand!

The Sweeper brushes with his broom,
  The Carstairs with his chalk
Retires—the Cripple leaves his stand,
  But cannot sell his walk.

The old Wall-blind resigns the wall,
  The Camels hide their humps,
The Witherington without a leg
  May n't beg upon his stumps!

Poor Jack is gone, that used to doff
  His battered tattered hat,
And show his dangling sleeve, alas!
  There seemed no arm in that!

Oh! it was such a sin to air
  His true blue naval rags,

Glory's own trophy, like St. Paul,
Hung round with holy flags!

Thou knowest best. I meditate,
My Bodkin, no offence!
Let us, henceforth, but guard our pounds,
Thou dost protect our pence!

Well art thou pointed 'gainst the Poor,
For, when the Beggar Crew
Bring their petitions, thou art paid,
Of course, to "run them through."

Doubtless thou art what Hamlet meant
To wretches the last friend:
What ills can mortals have, they can't
"With a bare *Bodkin*" end?

NOTES

TO THE ODES AND ADDRESSES.

ODE TO RICHARD MARTIN, ESQUIRE.

Mr. Martin was originally a gentleman of fortune, and was elected to represent the County of Galway in the first Parliament after the union of Great Britain and Ireland. He distinguished himself by his exertions for the passage of a bill to prevent cruelty to animals, and finally obtained an act of Parliament, which is known by his name. Whilst he continued in London, he was indefatigable in bringing before the magistrates cases in which it might be put into execution. He represented Galway in six Parliaments, but lost his election in 1826. He died at Boulogne, in France, in 1834, at the age of eighty years.

ADDRESS TO MR. DYMOKE, THE CHAMPION OF ENGLAND.

In the *London Magazine* for August, 1821, there is an account of the Coronation of George IV., in a "Letter from a Gentleman in Town to a Lady in the Country," of which the following is an extract.

"At the end of this course the gates of the Hall were again thrown open, and a noble flourish of trumpets announced to all eager hearts that the CHAMPION was about to enter. He advanced under the gateway, on a fine piebald charger, (an ill color,) and clad in complete steel. The plumes on his head were tri-colored, and extremely magnificent; and he bore in his hand the loose steel gauntlet, ready for challenge. The Duke of Wellington was on his right hand, the Marquis of Anglesea on his left. When he had come within the limits of the Hall, he was about to throw down his glove at once, so eager was he for the fray, but the Herald distinctly said, 'Wait till I have read the challenge,' and read it accordingly, the Champion husbanding his valor for a few minutes:

"'If any person, of what degree soever, high or low, shall deny or gainsay our Sovereign Lord King George the Fourth of the United Kingdom of Great Britain and Ireland, Defender of the Faith, son and next heir to our Sovereign Lord King George the Third, the last King deceased, to be right heir to the Imperial crown of the United Kingdom, or that he ought not to enjoy the same, here is his Champion who saith that he lieth, and is a false traitor; being ready in person to combat with him, and in this quarrel will adventure his life against him on what day soever he shall be appointed.'

"At the conclusion of this awful challenge, the Champion hurled down his gauntlet, which fell with a solemn clash upon the floor. It rang in most hearts! He then stuck his wrist against his steeled side, as though to show how indifferent he was to the consequence of his challenge. This certainly had a very pleasing and gallant effect. The Herald, in a few seconds, took up the glove, delivered it to the squire, who kissed it and handed it to the Champion. In the middle of the Hall the same ceremony was performed; and at the foot of the royal platform, it was a third time gone through. The King then drank his health, and methinks with real pleasure, for the Champion had right gallantly conducted himself. His Majesty then sent the cup to him; and he, taking it, drank to the King, but in so low a tone that I could only catch the meaning by the tumultuous shouts of the people. The noise seemed to awaken the courage of his horse, but he mastered his steed admirably. The ceremony of backing out of the Hall was then again performed, and successfully, with the exception of the Marquis of Anglesea's Arabian, whose doubts were not yet satisfied, and he was literally shown out by the pages."

In Hall's Account of the Coronation of Henry VIII. there is a passage, quoted by the writer in the *London Magazine*, describing the appearance in that ceremony of "Sir Robert Dimmoke, champion to the kynge by tenour of his enheritaunce." The office seems to have remained in the Dimmoke family till the time of George IV. At the Coronations of William IV. and Victoria, the Great Banquet, in the course of which it was usual for the Champion to appear, was omitted.

The following verses originally appeared in the *London Magazine* of September, 1821, p. 236.

THE CHAMPION'S FAREWELL.

Otium cum Dignitate.

Here! bring me my breeches, my armor is over;
  Farewell for some time to my tin pantaloons;
Double-milled kerseymere is a kind of leg clover,
  Good luck to broad cloth for a score or two moons!

Here! hang up my helmet, and reach me my beaver,
  This avoirdupois weight of glory must fall;
I think on my life that again I shall never
  Take my head in a sauce-pan to Westminster Hall.

Oh, why was my family born to be martial?
 'Tis a mercy this grand show-off-fight-day is up!
I do not think Cato was much over-partial
 To back through the dishes, with me and my cup.

By the blood of the Dymokes, I'll sit in my lodgings,
 And the gauntlet resign for "neat gentleman's doe;"
If I ride I *will* ride, and no longer be dodging
 My horse's own tail 'twixt Duke, Marquis & Co.

No more at my horsemanship folks shall make merry,
 For I'll ship man and horse, and "show off" not on shore;
No funnies for me! I will ride in a wherry;
 They feathered my skull, but I'll feather my oar.

So, Thomas, take Cato and put on his halter,
 And give him some beans, since I now am at peace;
If a Champion is wanted, pray go to Sir Walter,
 And he'll let you out Marmions at sovereigns apiece.

The ladies admired the piebald nag vastly,
 And clapped his old sober-sides into the street;
Here's a cheque upon Child, so, my man, go to Astley,
 Pay the charge of a charger, and take a receipt.

ODE TO JOSEPH GRIMALDI, SENIOR.

Grimaldi, the celebrated clown, took his final leave of the public at Drury Lane, in July, 1828. He was born in 1779, and died in 1837.

ODE TO CAPTAIN PARRY.

Sir William Edward Parry, a captain in the British navy, was born at Bath, December 19, 1790. He entered the navy in 1803, and distinguished himself in the blockade of Brest and in the Baltic during the war with Denmark. In 1811, he was sent to the Greenland seas for the protection of the British whale fishermen, and penetrated as far as the 76th degree of north latitude. In 1818, he commanded The Alexander, the second discovery ship in Captain Ross's northwest expedition. In 1819, he began a series of expeditions of discovery in the polar regions, which, under his command, were conducted with admirable skill. A complete account of these was published in 1833, under the title of "Four Voyages to the North Pole." The ode in the text was written on the occasion of Parry's third voyage.

ADDRESS TO MARIA DARLINGTON.

In December, 1824, an action was brought by the celebrated actress, Miss Foote, against Mr. Hayne, a gentleman of fortune, for a breach of promise of marriage. The Attorney-General stated that Miss Foote, while performing at the Cheltenham theatre, became acquainted with Colonel Berkeley, who, under a promise of marriage, seduced her, and she lived under his protection for five years. Two children were born; after the birth of the last, Miss Foote, finding that Colonel Berkeley did not fulfil his promise, resolved that the connection should cease. This was in June, 1824. Subsequently, she became engaged to Mr. Hayne. Colonel Berkeley, on learning of this engagement, communicated to Mr. Hayne the history of his connection with Miss Foote. Upon this, with Miss Foote's consent, Mr. Hayne withdrew from his engagement to marry her. He, afterwards, however, renewed his suit, and again was accepted. His second engagement he refused to fulfil. Upon which Miss Foote brought an action against him for breach of promise, and obtained three thousand pounds damages. Miss Foote married April 7, 1831, the Earl of Harrington, who died in 1851.

ODE TO W. KITCHENER, M. D.

The *London Magazine* for October, 1821, contains a review of Dr. Kitchener's *Cook's Oracle*, evidently written by Hood; and in the November number of the same journal is the following ode.

ODE TO DR. KITCHENER.

Ye Muses nine inspire,
And stir up my poetic fire;
Teach my burning soul to speak
With a bubble and a squeak!
Of Dr. Kitchener I fain would sing,
Till pots, and pans, and mighty kettles ring.

O culinary Sage!
(I do not mean the herb in use,
That always goes along with goose,)
How have I feasted on thy page!
"When like a lobster boiled, the morn
From black to red began to turn,"
Till midnight, when I went to bed,
And clapped my *tewah-diddle* [1] on my head.

Who is there cannot tell
Thou lead'st a life of living well?
"What baron, or squire, or knight of the shire,
Lives half so well as a holy Fry-er?"

In doing well thou must be reckon'd
The first, and Mrs. Fry the second;
And twice a Job—for in thy feverish toils,
Thou wast all over roasts, as well as boils.

Thou wast indeed no dunce,
To treat thy subjects and thyself at once.
Many a hungry poet eats
His brains like thee,
But few there be
Could live so long on their receipts.
What living soul or sinner
Would slight thy invitation to a dinner,
Ought with the Danaïdes to dwell,
Draw gravy in a cullender, and hear
For ever in his ear
The pleasant tinkling of thy dinner bell.

Immortal Kitchener! thy fame
Shall keep itself when Time makes game
Of other men's. Yea, it shall keep all weathers,
And thou shalt be upheld by thy pen-feathers.
Yea, by the sauce of Michael Kelly,
Thy name shall perish never,
But be magnified for ever,
By all whose eyes are bigger than their belly!

Yea, till the world is done
To a turn, and Time puts out the Sun,
Shall live the endless echo of thy name.
But as for thy more fleshy frame,
Oh, Death's carnivorous teeth will tittle
Thee out of breath, and eat it for cold victual.
But still thy fame shall be among the nations
Preserved to the last course of generations.

Ah, me! my soul is touched with sorrow
    To think how flesh must pass away;
    So mutton that is warm to-day
Is cold and turned to hashes on the morrow!
    Farewell! I would say more, but I
    Have other fish to fry.

ODE TO H. BODKIN, ESQ.

The Society for the Suppression of Mendicity was instituted in 1813. Mr. Bodkin, for many years its secretary, was very active in prosecution of beggars and vagabonds, and was, in consequence, severely lampooned by the press of London.

SONNETS.

I.

LITERARY REMINISCENCES.

Time was, I sat upon a lofty stool,
At lofty desk, and with a clerkly pen
Began each morning, at the stroke of ten,
To write in Bell and Co.'s commercial school;
In Warnford Court, a shady nook and cool,
The favourite retreat of merchant men;
Yet would my quill turn vagrant even then,
And take stray dips in the Castalian pool.
Now double entry — now a flowery trope —
Mingling poetic honey with trade wax —
Blogg, Brothers — Milton — Grote and Prescott —
Pope —
Bristles — and Hogg — Glyn Mills and Halifax —
Rogers — and Towgood — Hemp — the Bard of
Hope —
Barilla — Byron — Tallow — Burns — and Flax!

II.

TO A DECAYED SEAMAN.

Hail! seventy-four cut down! Hail, Top and Lop!
Unless I'm much mistaken in my notion,
Thou wast a stirring Tar, before that hop
Became so fatal to thy locomotion; —
Now, thrown on shore, like a mere weed of ocean,
Thou readest still to men a lesson good,
To King and Country showing thy devotion,
By kneeling thus upon a stump of wood!
Still is thy spirit strong as alcohol;
Spite of that limb, begot of acorn-egg,—
Methinks,— thou Naval History in one Vol.—
A virtue shines, e'en in that timber leg,
For unlike others that desert their Poll,
Thou walkest ever with thy "Constant Peg!"

III.

ON STEAM.

BY AN UNDER-OSTLER.

I WISH I livd a Thowsen year Ago
Wurking for Sober six and Seven milers
And dubble Stages runnen safe and slo
The Orsis cum in Them days to the Bilers
But Now by meens of Powers of Steem forces
A-turning Coches into Smoakey Kettels
The Bilers seam a Cumming to the Orses
And Helps and naggs Will sune be out of Vittels
Poor Bruits I wunder How we bee to Liv
When sutch a change of Orses is our Faits
No nothink need Be sifted in a Siv
May them Blowd ingins all Blow up their Grates
And Theaves of Oslers crib the Coles and Giv
Their blackgard Hannimuls a Feed of Slaits !

IV.

TO A SCOTCH GIRL, WASHING LINEN AFTER HER COUNTRY FASHION.

WELL done and wetly, thou Fair Maid of Perth:
  Thou mak'st a washing picture well deserving
  The pen and pencilling of Washington Irving:
Like dripping Naiad, pearly from her birth,
Dashing about the water of the Firth,
  To cleanse the calico of Mrs. Skirving,
  And never from thy dance of duty swerving
As there were nothing else than dirt on earth!
Yet what is thy reward? Nay, do not start!
  I do not mean to give thee a new damper,
But while thou fillest this industrious part
  Of washer, wearer, mangler, presser, stamper,
Deserving better character — thou art
  What Bodkin would but call — "a common tramper."

V.

TO LORD WHARNCLIFFE, ON HIS GAME-BILL.

I'm fond of partridges, I'm fond of snipes,
I'm fond of black cocks, for they 're very good cocks —
I'm fond of wild ducks, and I'm fond of woodcocks,
And grouse that set up such strange moorish pipes.
I'm fond of pheasants with their splendid stripes —
I'm fond of hares, whether from Whig or Tory —
I'm fond of capercailzies in their glory,—
Teal, widgeons, plovers, birds in all their types:
All these are in your care, Law-giving Peer,
And when you next address your Lordly Babel,
Some clause put in your Bill, precise and clear,
With due and fit provision to enable
A man that holds all kinds of game so dear
To keep, like Crockford, a good Gaming Table.

VI.

By R. M.

How sweet thus clad, in Autumn's mellow Tone,
With serious Eye, the russet Scene to view!
No Verdure decks the Forest, save alone
The sad green Holly, and the olive Yew.
The Skies, no longer of a garish Blue,
Subdued to Dove-like Tints, and soft as Wool,
Reflected show their slaty Shades anew
In the drab Waters of the clayey Pool.
Meanwhile yon Cottage Maiden wends to School,
In Garb of Chocolate so neatly drest,
And Bonnet puce, fit object for the Tool,
And chastened Pigments, of our Brother West;
Yea, all is silent, sober, calm, and cool,
Save gaudy Robin with his crimson Breast.

VII.

Allegory — A moral vehicle.— DICTIONARY.

I HAD a Gig-Horse, and I called him Pleasure,
  Because on Sundays, for a little jaunt,
He was so fast and showy, quite a treasure ;
  Although he sometimes kicked, and shied aslant.
I had a Chaise, and christened it Enjoyment,
  With yellow body, and the wheels of red,
Because 'twas only used for one employment,
  Namely, to go wherever Pleasure led.
I had a wife, her nickname was Delight ;
  A son called Frolic, who was never still :
Alas ! how often dark succeeds to bright !
  Delight was thrown, and Frolic had a spill,
Enjoyment was upset and shattered quite,
  And Pleasure fell a splitter on *Paine's Hill!*

VIII.

Along the Woodford road there comes a noise
Of wheels, and Mr. Rounding's neat postchaise
Struggles along, drawn by a pair of bays,
With Rev. Mr. Crow and six small Boys;
Who ever and anon declare their joys,
With trumping horns and juvenile huzzas,
At going home to spend their Christmas days,
And changing Learning's pains for Pleasure's toys.
Six weeks elapse, and down the Woodford way,
A heavy coach drags six more heavy souls,
But no glad urchins shout, no trumpets bray;
The carriage makes a halt, the gate-bell tolls,
And little Boys walk in as dull and mum
As six new scholars to the Deaf and Dumb.

IX.

WRITTEN IN A WORKHOUSE.

Oh, blessed ease! no more of heaven I ask:
  The overseer is gone — that vandal elf —
  And hemp, unpicked, may go and hang itself,
While I, untasked, except with Cowper's Task,
In blessed literary leisure bask,
  And lose the workhouse, saving in the works
  Of Goldsmiths, Johnsons, Sheridans, and
      Burkes;
Eat prose and drink of the Castalian flask;
The themes of Locke, the anecdotes of Spence,
  The humorous of Gay, the Grave of Blair —
Unlearned toil, unlettered labours hence!
  But, hark! I hear the master on the stair
And Thomson's Castle, that of Indolence,
  Must be to me a castle in the air.

X.

A SOMNAMBULIST.

" A change came o'er the spirit of my dream." — BYRON.

METHOUGHT — for Fancy is the strangest gadder
When sleep all homely mundane ties hath riven —
Methought that I ascended Jacob's ladder,
With heartfelt hope of getting up to heaven :
Some bell, I knew not whence, was sounding seven
When I set foot upon that long one-pair ;
And still I climbed when it had chimed eleven
Nor yet of landing-place became aware ;
Step after step in endless flight seemed there ;
But on, with steadfast hope, I struggled still,
To gain that blessed haven from all care,
Where tears are wiped, and hearts forget their ill,
When, lo ! I wakened on a sadder stair —
Tramp — tramp — tramp — tramp — upon the Brixton Mill !

XI.

TO VAUXHALL.

"The English Garden." — MASON.

THE cold transparent ham is on my fork —
It hardly rains — and hark the bell ! — ding-dingle —
Away ! Three thousand feet at gravel work,
Mocking a Vauxhall shower ! — Married and Single
Crush — rush ; — Soaked Silks with wet white Satin mingle.
Hengler ! Madame ! round whom all bright sparks lurk,
Calls audibly on Mr. and Mrs. Pringle
To study the Sublime, &c. — (*vide* Burke)
All Noses are upturned ! — Whish — ish ! — On high
The rocket rushes — trails — just steals in sight —
Then droops and melts in bubbles of blue light —
And Darkness reigns — Then balls flare up and die —
Wheels whiz — smack crackers — serpents twist — and then
Back to the cold transparent ham again !

XII.

THE sky is glowing in one ruddy sheet;—
A cry of fire! resounds from door to door;
And westward still the thronging people pour;—
The turncock hastens to F. P. 6 feet,
And quick unlocks the fountains of the street;
While rumbling engines, with increasing roar,
Thunder along to luckless Number Four,
Where Mr. Dough makes bread for folks to eat.
And now through blazing frames, and fiery beams,
The Globe, the Sun, the Phœnix, and what not,
With gushing pipes throw up abundant streams,
On burning bricks, and twists, on rolls—too hot—
And scorching loaves,—as if there were no shorter
And cheaper way of making toast-and-water!

www.ingramcontent.com/pod-product-compliance
Lightning Source LLC
LaVergne TN
LVHW010228110826
845151LV00004B/1220

* 9 7 8 1 4 2 5 5 2 6 9 7 9 *